Appreciat
A Buddhist (

T0273059

Prajnaketu has written a deeply thoughtful, nuanced contemporary account of how Buddhists can relate to their digital life. Rather than offering simple solutions based on harking back to a now vanished, pre-Internet past, he accepts that the digital landscape is an inescapable part of our lives in the twenty-first century, and offers a wide-ranging critique of how we can best navigate this new world.

Brave, honest, and beautifully written, Prajnaketu has tremendous skill in articulating key teachings of the Buddha in highly accessible, witty, self-revealing ways. Rather than trotting out statements assuming we can match high ideals, his starting place is the way we actually live as humans – messy at times, addicted at times – and he offers a range of reflections about how we might bring all of this into our Buddhist practice as we learn to navigate the cyberloka. He courageously tackles the taboos of sex and porn and his chapter on the *Facebook Sutta* is simply brilliant. – **Vidyamala Burch**, author of *Mindfulness for Health* and *Mindfulness for Women*, and Co-Founder of The Breathworks Foundation

Prajnaketu knows from experience the deep, restorative value of awareness and positive emotion when it comes to facing the new kinds of challenges inherent in an online world. His non-judgemental, unfailingly kind, and witty engagement with the thornier aspects of the Web promotes open-ended dialogue with the reader, recognizing each of us as a responsible, potentially enlightened agent of our own destiny in relation to social media and the Internet as it morphs around us. Whatever views we hold about the Web's impact on our mental and spiritual health, this is a fundamentally encouraging and human-centred book that helps seed some important conversations for anyone practising as a Buddhist today. – **Candradasa**, Founding Director of Free Buddhist Audio and The Buddhist Centre Online, and author of *Buddhism for Teens*

An engagingly personal dialogue between Buddhism and how to survive life in the metaverse. Read it and be enlightened! – **Robin Dunbar**, Professor, University of Oxford

Sean Parker, the first president of Facebook, claimed that social networks are exploiting human vulnerability, saying: 'God only knows what it's doing to our children's brains.' We may never get to hear what God thinks about it, but Prajnaketu offers a clear-sighted and refreshing Buddhist critique of our digital lives, free from dogma and moralizing. Besides this, we now have a new sutta – the *Facebook Sutta* – to guide us. So next time I'm in a social media nosedive, I'll take a moment of self-awareness to ask: Why am I on social media anyway? – **Shantigarbha**, activist, mediator and author of *The Burning House: A Buddhist Response to the Climate and Ecological Emergency* and *I'll Meet You There: A Practical Guide to Empathy, Mindfulness and Communication*

We do it a lot, but don't talk about it much. In this book Prajnaketu doesn't tell us *what* to think, instead he teaches us *how* to think about the ethics of our Internet use. *Cyberloka* is the Buddhist guide that's been waiting to be written! – **Subhadramati**, author of *Not About Being Good: A Practical Guide to Buddhist Ethics*

CYBERLOKA

PRAJNAKETU

CYBERLOKA

A BUDDHIST GUIDE TO DIGITAL LIFE

Windhorse Publications
38 Newmarket Road
Cambridge CB5 8DT
info@windhorsepublications.com
windhorsepublications.com

Cover design by Katarzyna Manecka
Cover image: Łukasz Rawa/Unsplash

Typesetting and layout Tarajyoti
Printed by Bell & Bain Ltd, Glasgow

British Library Cataloguing in Publication Data:
A catalogue record for this book is available from the British Library.

ISBN 978-1-911407-92-8

Contents

Contents

About the author

Prajnaketu was born Timothy Holden in 1985 in Southampton, England. A keen meditator from the age of sixteen, he began to embrace Buddhism while studying for a degree in mathematics and philosophy at the University of Oxford. After teaching mathematics in two challenging schools, he co-founded the Oxford Triratna Buddhist Centre, where he currently works. He previously ran a Europe-wide network of young Buddhists for five years.

He was ordained into the Triratna Buddhist Order in 2014 and given the name Prajnaketu, 'he who holds a lamp of wisdom'. Living with his partner in Oxford, he currently directs the Urgyen Sangharakshita Trust and is one of Sangharakshita's literary executors. He's at his most inspired when reflecting, writing, and teaching at the interface between Buddhism and twenty-first-century life.

Author's acknowledgements

I'd like to thank the many people who read and offered their thoughts on early drafts of the material that became this book: Shantiprabha, Saddhaloka, Candradasa, Sadayasihi, Danayutta, Prasadacarin, and the readers at Windhorse Publications among others. Dhammamegha's warm and intelligent input has made editing this book both a learning process and a joy. Thanks to Michelle and Dhatvisvari at Windhorse for their clear-headed and supportive efforts at turning my rough manuscript into the book you are now reading. I'm also very grateful to Ellie, my partner, for her wholehearted encouragement of my writing projects, as well as her remarkable patience, love, and grounding humour as I've lived through some of the episodes I reflect on here. I thank Brenda and Geoff, my parents, for their great generosity throughout my life, not least in bankrolling many new generations of devices that have made these reflections possible. Finally, I acknowledge an unpayable debt of gratitude to Urgyen Sangharakshita, my Buddhist teacher, from whom I derive my inspiration to practise Buddhism and apply it to my life. Every reflection of value in this book comes directly or indirectly from him.

Publisher's acknowledgements

Windhorse Publications wishes to gratefully acknowledge a grant from the Future Dharma Fund and the Triratna European Chairs' Assembly Fund towards the production of this book.

We also wish to acknowledge and thank the individual donors who gave to the book's production via our 'Sponsor-a-book' campaign.

Introduction

You started out with such good intentions. Maybe you were going to thank your auntie for her lovely gift. Or just check the forecast to see if you'd need an umbrella for later. But you've just spent the last half an hour scrolling down the comments on a video that's now a distant memory. Your shoulders are tense, your eyes are bleary, and you feel vaguely angry in a can't-quite-put-my-finger-on-it way. Oh, and you've just missed your bus stop.

Welcome to the cyberloka.

This book is for human beings who use the Internet. Whether the above scenario is familiar or not, I'm sure we've all encountered what I call the *cyberloka* – the realm of online activity, *screen time* – and its effects. 'Cyberloka' is a made-up term combining 'cyber', adapted from Greek to refer to electronic communication, and 'loka', a Sanskrit word meaning 'world of experience'. For Buddhists, as we'll see, a loka is not a brute fact 'out there': what appears as the objective situation *arises together* with our minds. This teaching says we're constantly co-creating the worlds that we inhabit along with our family and social conditioning, the previous choices we've made, and the products of our imagination. This co-creation has a sort of 'logic', consisting of the cyclical patterns we fall into, and the seemingly objective landmarks in that realm – all of which hang together as a piece. The

1

message at the heart of this book is that it's helpful to look at our relationship to digital technology in the same way – as if it ushers in a new realm: the cyberloka. We can think of the cyberloka, then, as the world of experience – our thoughts, feelings, actions, habits, relationships, and more – that we co-create with digital technology.

This is more than just a theoretical interest to me. Like everyone of my generation, the story of my life, from childhood to adulthood, *just is* the story of how these technologies went from being distinct things that helped us to log onto (or self-consciously 'surf') the Internet, through to the ether in which many of us spend the majority of our lives. Even to speak of our 'digital lives' as if that refers to something distinct from the rest of our lives isn't quite right: *our lives are now inescapably digital.*

How we navigate this realm, then, has existential consequences for us. It really may mark the difference between mindlessly scrolling our way into old age, or making the most of this precious human life. I'm certainly no stranger to getting things wrong, and I draw on many of my own misadventures in the reflections that fill the following pages. At the same time, I've seen how Buddhism offers insights that help us to not only manage our digital lives, but even *flourish* in them.

But this is not a book of Buddhist digital dos and don'ts. There is plenty of good advice around on how to improve our use of the Internet.[1] While we will occasionally visit cyber-hygiene and cyber-McMindfulness in this book, they won't

---

1 See, for example, the Center for Humane Technology, available at https://www.humanetech.com/, accessed on 7 February 2022.

detain us. Buddhism is much more about discerning the principles that help us to live the best possible lives, and then living them out. Fundamentally, it boils down to one of the earliest Buddhist teachings:

> Experiences are preceded by mind, led by mind, and produced by mind. If one speaks or acts with an impure mind, suffering follows even as the cart wheel follows the hoof of the ox (drawing the cart).

> Experiences are preceded by mind, led by mind, and produced by mind. If one speaks or acts with a pure mind, happiness follows like a shadow that never departs.[2]

We're going to explore what these verses mean for our inevitably digital lives. One of the many things that these words convey is the centrality of our minds in all that we experience. Of course, there are objective factors that come into play too, but at base it's our minds that shape how our experience unfolds. This is as true in face-to-face interactions as it is over social media. But I've not yet come across any systematic attempt to apply these ideas in the digital arena.

It may come as a surprise that Buddhism has something substantial to say here other than: 'Avoid!' Sure enough, the Buddha taught a path of increasing simplicity and disentanglement from 'worldly pursuits' – and for many Buddhists it doesn't get any worldlier than the Internet. Time away from their screens is undoubtedly going to be an ingredient in the life of any remotely serious meditation practitioner. But to

---

2 *Dhammapada: The Way of Truth*, trans. Sangharakshita, Windhorse Publications, Cambridge 2011, chapter 1, verses 1–2, p.13.

place an unqualified total prohibition on screen time is, I feel, a missed opportunity. Yes, the cyberloka can be a realm of distraction, complexity, and even acrimony at times. But the Buddhist tradition, in the form of its teaching of the Wheel of Life and what I call its 'two ethics', offers us a template for not only ameliorating these aspects of the cyberloka, but even liberating ourselves and others from its downsides.

In this book, we're going to open up the cyberloka to this Buddhist perspective, looking especially at our data diets, sex, and social media.[3] The structure of the book follows my own tumbles into the cyberloka over the years: beginning with my tentative boyhood exposure to the static pages of Web 1.0,[4] taking in my ignoble experiences of pornography as a student, and moving into my professional exchanges with others on social media. Chapter 1, then, reflects on how we might discern what is of value in the cornucopia of information, media, texts, teachings – in short, *data* – that are now ever so available to us, and how to relate to them in order to help us transform our lives, rather than just skate along its surface. Chapter 2 brings into the daylight a long-overdue conversation between Buddhist ethics and the shadowy world of porn. Chapter 3 then imagines how the Buddha might have engaged with social media, looking at better ways to use opportunities for multidirectional communication and how to help others to do so.

---

3 There are lots of other topics worth covering – shopping, gaming, working, and dating are four that come to mind straight away – but no account could be exhaustive. Nevertheless, I believe that the principles we'll uncover will adapt straightforwardly to existing (and novel) areas, with a little imagination.
4 Named retrospectively at the advent of Web 2.0.

There will also be questions for reflection and discussion. This is the real point of the book. In a way, my own reflections – however inspired and insightful, or problematic – are merely prompts to help you enquire into *your* experiences and to open up sensible conversations. Only by engaging with this process will we begin to act from our best online. So my strong advice would be to reflect on each short section *thoroughly* before moving on to the next. A rough-and-ready suggestion would be to spend at least twice as long reflecting as reading. Perhaps this is an unusual request, but, rather than being a body of knowledge to acquire, Buddhist insights absorb slowly into our systems: reading, reflecting, making mistakes, talking them over, and eventually acting with greater freedom. This process will take much longer than the time you spend reading my thoughts.

Before we begin with those thoughts, though, it's worth acknowledging two trends that appear in most discussions around technology, or, for that matter, anything new. After all, the digital age is still, even in the scheme of individual lives, and especially the grand sweep of human history, relatively new. So much so that some people speak of a 'digital revolution' having taken place over the last twenty years or so. Such revolutions, as we can witness from the political and sexual revolutions of the twentieth century, bring out a spectrum of responses. At one pole stand those who embrace the revolution, and at the other those who resist it. Each pole brings its own gifts and burdens to the discussion. The embracers' openness to new possibilities allows for creativity and the attractive energy of experimentation and play. They can also often suffer from a degree of naivety and shortsightedness, and can adopt an evangelical zeal bordering on insensitivity. The resisters, however, are aware of the valuable lessons of the past and bring a sceptical wisdom to the developments they see unfolding before them. At the same time, their scepticism can mean they miss opportunities, lapse into moralizing, and risk tarnishing their cherished values with heaviness, weariness, and irrelevancy as times move on. Most of us can probably recognize the pull of both tendencies at various times in our lives. And it's instructive that even some of the highest-profile agents of the digital revolution have come out as its most vocal critics.[5]

This book is unlikely to gratify those at either pole. Buddhist practice culminates in wisdom and compassion: inseparable qualities that combine ancient values and creative applications, realism with a joyful desire to benefit others. I'm curious about how we cultivate these qualities in the realm of digital technology. And, as we'll see, I've been around the Internet enough times now to be confident that it is worth attempting to chart a middle way between and above these poles.

The second trend involves the perils of writing a *book* – the most static medium – on a theme as dynamic as digital technology. Tech dates rapidly: it doesn't take long for what once elicited desire and even awe to pass into familiarity (as it hits the mainstream), overfamiliarity (as it mulches into our

---

5 Take Sean Parker, the first president of the social network Facebook, who has claimed that social networks deliberately exploit human vulnerabilities and who wonders: 'God only knows what it's doing to our children's brains.' See https://www.businessinsider. nl/apple-ceo-tim-cook-doesnt-let-nephew-use-social-media-2018-1/, accessed on 7 February 2022.

clichés and assumptions), satire (like the joke about the man who returned to his car after realizing he'd left his Nokia on the passenger seat only to find the window broken and *two* Nokias), pity (as when I revealed my vintage[6] small-screened iPhone to my Indian friends), nostalgia, and eventually obscurity and oblivion. If technology dates rapidly, books about technology are often obsolete before they've even hit the shelf. So it's with some humility around this that I illustrate what I say with contemporary examples.

I also draw (currently meaningful) distinctions between social media and the rest of the Internet, our (handheld) devices and our bodies, reality and *virtual* reality – all of which may well go the way of previously meaningful, though now rather quaint, distinctions such as online/offline or even on/ off (as I discovered to my bafflement recently in attempting to locate a dedicated power button). Linked with this is the danger of writing about attitudes while they're still forming – it may well be that before long the 'insights' here will have become truisms, simply because our collective digital culture has matured. Time may also reveal the naivety in my notes of optimism.

We can't predict the ways in which technological or social trends will evolve. Though our attitudes to them will likely follow the process described above, the basic motivating principle of this book – of bringing curiosity to the interactions between our minds and new technology, in whatever forms it takes – will undoubtedly remain relevant long into the future.

---

6 A euphemism used by the digital hardware and software company Apple to describe hardware it no longer considers when designing new software.

As human beings, we will continue to reflect on our digital lives so long as we live them. My wish in writing this book is that my reflections will spark off reflections in you. The digital world is with us to stay; how we live in it – in the fullest, Buddhist, sense – is the question we'll hopefully continue to ask, even as its specifics evolve. This guide is here to help us bring some of the Buddha's wisdom to bear on this unfolding process.

Questions for reflection and discussion

What areas of your digital life do you particularly want to shed a light on?

How will you keep these in mind as you read and reflect on this book?

1

Hyperavailability, data diets, and depth

In Oxford, the city where I live, there's a bookshop called Blackwell's. On entering, it looks like a fairly ordinary independent bookshop. Keep going and you realize that the small front room extends deeper into the building. Go down the stairs and the shop opens up into a veritable cavern, filled with books of all kinds. I vividly recall visiting Blackwell's at around the age of four – the seemingly ever-expanding rooms of books conjuring up fantasies of an erudite Bond villain's underground lair.

On returning to the shop again as a student in my late teens, what struck me instead was a tension – a tension born of the aspiring scholar in me. On the one hand was the availability of so much information, knowledge, and maybe even wisdom; on the other was the certainty that I would never be able to read it all. Not even close. And more new books would arrive every day than I'd be able to read in a year. What dawned on me was that, in the face of this quantity of literature, I would need to choose what to read – to discern what was, and what wasn't, worth reading – and, actually, I didn't know where to start.

Of course, this was outside the cyberloka. But by the time I became a student I'd already encountered this *in* the cyberloka (à la Web 1.0), where I felt the tension multiplied manyfold. Whether it was shopping for consumer (i.e. real-life) goods, watching pixelated videos and downloading music, accessing information, catching up on news, listening to spiritual teachings, or simply receiving messages from my friends, the cyberloka was a realm of the *hyperavailable*. By hyperavailability, I'm not just referring to the fact that there's lots of stuff we can access online. Though of course there is. I mean as well that we can access it very quickly – sometimes instantly – and certainly much more quickly than previous generations could.

This is a key element of the 'logic' of the cyberloka: heaps of novel information, only a scroll or a (hyper)link away. This plays into our basic human reward systems involving dopaminergic neurons, cells in the brain that produce the neurotransmitter dopamine. As neuroscientist Tali Sharot puts it:

> Dopamine is released when we expect a reward and when we receive an unexpected reward [...] [and] it turns out that it is also released when we expect information and when we unexpectedly receive information [...] [W]e are driven to seek information by the same neural principles that drive us to seek water, nourishment, and sex.[7]

So you can imagine my excitement as, aged eleven, I logged onto the computer at my local library for the first time. I'd booked a slot in advance for the one machine that was connected to the Internet. And, as I dutifully followed my list of things to look up, I could see that the wealth of information and the speed at which I could access it (compared to looking in reference books or asking people

7 Tali Sharot, *The Influential Mind*, Little, Brown, London 2017, pp.112–13.

around me) were opening up a *new way of life*. By present-day standards this wasn't anything visually spectacular, being mostly static pages of text. And yet I was thrilled by what this made possible for me. At the time, I could hardly have imagined the superabundance of information that would emerge over the coming decades.

On the face of it, this availability is surely a good thing. Scarcity and delay have been the scourges of previous generations (and still continue to be for many people across the world). In the domain of spiritual teachings, for example, there are legendary accounts of Buddhist practitioners having to make long and dangerous journeys to acquire new teachings. In the 1960s, the Eastern texts translated into English were few and far between – so much so that it was possible to keep abreast of most of the new developments in the world of Buddhist literature. This just isn't our experience now: if there's a book I want, I can get it delivered the next day, find a PDF version online, or, better still, find a podcast interview with the author and not have to bother with the book at all.

Here, and in Chapter 2, I want to explore my earliest encounters with the cyberloka, which were primarily as a *consumer*. At the time – in my teenage years and slightly before – I had neither the know-how nor the inclination to publish Web pages, which, as I recall, was a niche pursuit anyway. It wasn't until the advent of social media (also known as Web 2.0) that ascending to the status of a content *creator* became easier, and in time the norm. But more on that in Chapter 3.

Even going back to the late 1990s, we had so many options for what to watch, read, listen to, buy, rent, download, or save for later. And yet, with the benefit of a lot of hindsight, simply gorging ourselves on this buffet of data doesn't seem to be the way to go. Maybe that's obvious enough. These days, I'm getting better at realizing that allowing my attention to be directed by what's 'up next' is likely to result in feeling empty, frustrated, and unable to sleep.

The ethics of restraint

This is where the first main area of Buddhist ethics, as I see it, comes in. The word 'ethics' in itself is likely to have different associations for different people – some rather problematic, I'm sure. I'm not going to go into detail on this – to do so would involve a whole collection of books – but speaking very broadly we can tease out two trends of ethical teachings within the Buddhist tradition that, in my view, add considerable value to our ordinary Western understanding of ethics. First, there's the ethics of *restraint*; then, the ethics of *altruism*.[8]

The ethics of restraint appears in the *five precepts*: training principles to refrain from taking life, taking the not-given, sexual misconduct, false speech, and intoxication. These are the bedrock of Buddhist ethical practice, and the Buddha recommends them as the basis for meditation as well as the arising of wisdom. While they do have an other-regarding dimension to them, the emphasis is often on how refraining from these acts benefits us: clarifying our conscience and preparing our minds to see things as they really are. This became known as the *Arahant Ideal*, the arahant being a

---

8 Which we'll return to in Chapter 2.

follower of the Buddha's teaching who gains enlightenment primarily with themselves in mind.[9]

Translating this into the idiom of realms, the ethics of restraint is about ceasing to react in the ways that lock us into a realm of suffering. Because we remain in any realm only so long as we act in particular ways, by refraining from the characteristic attitudes and behaviours of the realm we're in, we free ourselves from it. Putting it another way, the ethics of restraint is a matter of releasing ourselves from unhelpful habits, as a preparation for becoming our best. We'll return later to an aspect of what this 'best' might mean under the heading of *depth*. For the time being, when it comes to hyperavailability in the cyberloka, suffice it to say that I have plenty of experience of it *not* leading to depth.

How *not* to relate to hyperavailability: Two case studies

Having been born in the mid-1980s, I grew up alongside the digital revolution. Kids and younger adults are often at the forefront of understanding and adopting technological innovations, and my life has coincided with one of the richest periods of innovation in human history. One of the benefits of the phase of growing up is that we're given permission to embrace new things and make mistakes. And, provided the mistakes aren't too big, we also have a chance to learn from them. So, putting it another way, I've also been at the forefront of making mistakes in relation to these new technologies. And

---

9 Though there is no shortage of commentators who point out the contradiction in the notion of a self-centred pursuit of a selfless goal.

occasionally I've learned from them. The next two sections are mostly about the mistakes.

iTunes, your tunes, MyTunes ... no tunes!

When I was growing up, music was a huge part of my life. My dad was a piano teacher and choirmaster, and it was from him that I learned how to play the piano and sing. There was always music in our home – from Bach's fugues to church hymns to *Sounds of the Sixties*[10] on a Saturday morning. Studying music for my high-school exams, I was exposed to the spectrum of Western music and, as I developed my own tastes, amassed a sizeable and eclectic collection of CDs,[11] at least by the standards of my friendship group at the time.

Within the first few weeks of starting university I came to realize that my knowledge of music up to that point was in fact rather paltry. I found there was so much more music out there, though only by a happy accident. One day I noticed that plugging my Microsoft Windows[12] version of iTunes (still in its relative infancy) into the college's local area network granted me access to all the music of everyone else on the network. My fellow students included jazz musicians and world-class choristers – with huge collections. My pool of available music grew a hundredfold overnight. This meant not only that I was

---

10 A BBC Radio 2 programme focusing on pop music from the 1960s.
11 Compact discs – circular 'digital optical disc data storage' mediums of about 12 cm in diameter and providing capacity for up to 80 minutes of uncompressed audio. See 'Compact disc', available at https://en.wikipedia.org/wiki/Compact_disc, accessed on 7 February 2022.
12 An operating system for personal computers.

suddenly relieved of the need to buy music, but also that I could explore works that, through ignorance or prejudice, I'd never listened to before – and discover that some of it was really worth listening to.

However, there was a catch: as soon as my fellow students went offline, the possibilities for streaming ended. A minor downside, perhaps. So the music was available, yes, but not exactly *hyper*available. That was, until I discovered a handy little program called MyTunes.[13] This enabled me – and, as it turns out, a large number of other college students in the early 2000s – to circumvent the restrictions placed on iTunes and download every single track on the network. Before long, the modest 30 gigabytes of my laptop's hard disk were bulging with *weeks'* worth of music. I imagined I would never be in want of music ever again.

But pretty soon I realized that something had changed in my relation to the music I now 'owned'. Whereas previously I would listen to whole albums at a time, often many times over, lovingly acquainting myself with their nuances, now I found myself restlessly skipping from one artist or one track to the next, sometimes even before having finished what I was listening to. My listening style had suddenly gone from an intimacy born of limited options only weeks before to a disorienting array of quality tunes with which I was to have, at best, only a momentary fling. It was a strange experience – I had so much exquisite music at my fingertips, and yet the more I had, the less I seemed to value it. I was aware of this at the time, and I came to link it to the notion of 'shuffle mode'

---

13 'MyTunes', available at https://en.wikipedia.org/wiki/MyTunes, accessed on 7 February 2022.

– the definitions of shuffle involving things like 'restlessly shift[ing] one's position' and 'look[ing] through (a number of things) hurriedly',[14] none of which felt like a satisfactory or desirable way to relate to music. In fact, most of what I downloaded I never got around to listening to: in the paralysis of choice I then experienced, I found myself gravitating to what I had previously – genuinely, legally – owned and largely overlooking the new stuff.

It's a testament to the lack of value I associated with this wealth of music that a couple of years later, when reformatting my hard disk, I completely forgot about my collection and destroyed it forever. I never regretted this or sought to restore it after its demise. The novelty of hyperavailable music had, perhaps, worn off.

My 'spiritual awakening'

I experienced something similar in the arena of spiritual teachings. I'd been brought up in the Church of England, regularly attending my local church, singing in the choir, and being a loyal member of that community for all of my childhood and adolescence. When I was around fifteen or sixteen, things began to change. I began to question Christianity more intensely, started studying philosophy, and embarked on a meditation practice, which I've continued to this day. One of the things I found dissatisfying about that spiritual context – wholesome, culturally rich, and benign though it was – was the lack of spiritual depth that I perceived in its teachings and its proponents. In

---

14 *Concise Oxford Dictionary*, 11th ed., ed. Catherine Soanes and Angus Stevenson, Oxford University Press, Oxford 2004, p.1336.

particular, I was longing to explore my own mind and its relation to Reality in meditation, and I simply found no one with whom to discuss this. It just didn't seem to be a thing. What's more, my school friends already thought I was weird enough, and I wasn't going to give them further cause for concern, so I didn't talk to them about my interests either. I went it alone.

So for six or seven years I explored spiritual matters in a solitary mode: I learned meditation from a book, kept a journal, meditated on my own, and tried to make sense of my experience as best I could. Then I discovered, in the days of Web 1.0, the growing corpus of spiritual material online, mostly in long-form text: stories of Sri Ramakrishna, Sufi poetry and its commentaries, a few translations of Buddhist canonical literature, quotes from various Hindu 'babas' and swamis, testimonies of Transcendental Meditation practitioners, and information on Goenka's Vipassana retreats. The latter seemed to hold something of an allure for me – the idea of going on a by-donation, silent meditation retreat appealed – and at the time I regularly read and reread the literature around it all (which was very limited, the only updates being the six-monthly announcements of upcoming retreats). Strange to say, though, and true to my timid teenage self, I never actually went on one of these retreats. Perhaps it was simply my shyness at the time. Perhaps also there was something about it that didn't seem quite right to me. (I still haven't been on one, though I've attended many other retreats.)

From that cornucopia of spiritual media – still rather modest by today's standards – I valiantly attempted to synthesize a personal path of practice as well as a coherent philosophical system to make sense of it all. I failed. By the time I wound up at the university Buddhist Society, aged twenty-one, I was both superficially knowledgeable and confused, and I'd exhausted my hopes of finding inspiration online. I'd arrived at the fact that I was no longer a Christian – which perhaps in itself was progress – but I didn't really know who I was or what I was doing.

Partly, I took pride in what I saw as a transcending of labels and a sloughing off of the strictures of that bogeyman, Organized Religion. But increasingly I was coming to realize that going it alone and trying to cobble something together out of the myriad – often conflicting – voices that I met in the cyberloka weren't going to work for me. I've heard a similar story countless times from other people down the years too: probably most of us come to ground in our attempts to deal with the hyperavailability of spiritual resources online.

* * *

These are just two of the areas in which hyperavailability has tripped me up. What I find curious is that, in both cases, the content was intrinsically valuable – it represented some of the best of what humanity had to offer in the realms of music and spirituality. But I came unstuck in the way I was relating to so much content. And the major casualty in all of this was depth.

Questions for reflection and discussion

When did you first experience hyperavailability?

How did it change how you related to information for better or for worse?

What have you done differently as a result?

What is depth?

Looking at it through the eyes of a poet, depth is a vertical metaphor: going down into something, to its roots, its origins, its foundations. It also connotes the bottom of the oceans and the mysterious vistas and life forms that one might meet there. Depth is about the process of transitioning to a different way of being, one that is simpler and closer to the core of life. Depth frees us from the unhelpful habits that we can fall into; suddenly life opens up to us again. We could contrast this vertical metaphor with a horizontal one. If depth disrupts our habits by plunging beneath them to what matters – to what we *really* want – horizontality might mean continuing in the habitual grooves of our minds, just now with more stuff. Horizontality can also mean we treat everything we encounter as occupying the same level. Whether it's a video of the Dalai Lama giving a profound teaching or 'gymnast vs bodybuilder pull-up competition' – if it all appears to us on the same little screen, the temptation is to treat it as somehow equal in value, even if, in our more lucid moments, we know that it isn't.

And horizontality connotes a spreading out, or proliferating, or accumulating of more of the same, rather than a qualitative shift in experience.

Digestion is another suitable image for depth: the food we consume going down into the stomach and bowels, and from there being absorbed into the fabric of our bodies. It also illustrates what can go wrong with many of the ways we relate to hyperavailable phenomena. In the same way that we might overeat our favourite food if given half a chance, we're so prone to overconsuming what's hyperavailable. In overeating, we initially get indigestion and, if we make a habit of it, we put on weight. Well, it's fair to say that most of us are information-obese – not knowing when to stop, even when our minds are flabby and stuffed with data. Sometimes we don't even realize until we stop consuming information – say, on a residential retreat – quite how much we've been taking on.

In the same way as eating healthily – which itself is not a straightforward proposition for many of us – we'd do well to find balance and moderation in our data diets, and offer our minds more time to digest what we've consumed. So far, so much just ordinary good mental hygiene. But this chapter goes beyond merely keeping us healthy – depth, as I see it, is perhaps the greatest and most radical gift that Buddhism has to offer. Depth is, in a word, *freedom*. Freedom to stand outside the habitual, predictable, cycles of the realm we're in, even if only temporarily, at which point its power over us begins to wane. So it's essential that we're able to recognize depth when we experience it, and know how to develop it.

An experience of depth

One of the boons of being a practising Buddhist, in a spiritually vital Order, is that I regularly happen upon experiences of depth, and even of deepening depth. So much of what my community does is geared around creating moments, hours, months, and even lifetimes of greater depth for people. I've never found anything quite like it anywhere else. And what's more, the depth we cultivate in explicitly Buddhist settings translates to other settings too – I get loads more out of concerts, films, and conversations now I've learned how to tap more into this key aspect of human life.

But to illustrate what depth might look like, I'll stick with an example from my Buddhist practice. Most years, lockdowns notwithstanding, I've been going on a retreat over Christmas and New Year to a men's retreat centre, Padmaloka, on the outskirts of a village in Norfolk. Leaving behind the chilly platforms of Norwich bus station, its tinny PA system warbling out Mariah Carey and Slade's Christmas hits, we travel along unlit roads, passing the occasional decorated house, until we enter the Norfolk Broads.

It's quiet – deeply quiet – the faint glow of activity inside the retreat centre buildings flickering towards us as we pass through the main gate. This annual retreat takes place mostly in silence and for men who are members of our Order or who are training to join it. After a few days of teaching input, one or two hours of talking per day, we then plunge into more than a week of continuous silence, meditation, and ritual. We switch our phones and other devices off and, before long, forget all about them. The leaders even discourage us from reading, except sparingly and for inspiration. The food is simple and tasty. We take walks at a local nature reserve, the wildlife dormant or flown south. Life is quiet, simple, regular.

Every evening after dinner, we meditate in the main shrine room – a room whose walls teem with images of various figures from the Buddhist pantheon: Buddhas, bodhisattvas, historical and legendary characters. As the lights dim, the main image of the historical Buddha, Shakyamuni, takes centre stage. All that's left of the other images is their benevolent presence supporting us from afar. After the meditation we do a ritual, normally one based on an epic poem by the eighth-century philosopher-poet Santideva, in seven parts. The whole ritual builds to the point where we're ready to hear a reading from an enlightened mind – from a mind of boundless depth. I recall vividly on one retreat a teaching from Kukai, a Japanese Zen master, writing to a nobleman in Kyoto about his decision to remain in the mountains meditating rather than come to the city:

Have you not seen, O have you not seen,
This has been man's fate; how can you alone live forever?
Thinking of this, my heart always feels torn;
You, too, are like the sun going down in the western
    mountains,
Or a living corpse whose span of life is nearly over.
Futile would be my stay in the capital;
Away, away, I must go, I must not stay there.[15]

---

15 From *Kukai: Major Works*, trans. Yoshito S. Hakeda, Columbia University Press, New York 1972, p.51.

This has been man's fate. These words are etched in my memory – words of a man who deeply understood the human condition and lived out that understanding to its fullest. The contrast with my own life of busyness, taking for granted that one day of youth and activity will always be followed by the next, rings throughout my conscience. I feel chastened and inspired. Moved. Tingles, beginning at the base of my spine, rise up and spread across my shoulders: an ecstatic energy that crashes like waves again and again over me, only to subside and leave me in a state of beautiful, blissful, peace.

As I begin to become more aware of the others in the shrine room around me, I notice the profound stillness as they listen to the reading – not a single shuffle or clearing of the throat. I can only conclude that my own experience is part of a collective aesthetic shift, a mutual deepening, born of the efforts we've been making, day in, day out, in silence together on this retreat.

When I talk about depth, this is what I mean: a wordless, supra-personal movement towards beauty and truth that seems to alter the fabric of our reality for the better. It would be my greatest wish fulfilled if more people could tap into this kind of thing. But it's rare, and perhaps increasingly rare – and we generally need help to access it. We might start by asking ourselves: have we had moments like these before? And if so, what conditions gave rise to them?

We ask these questions not to try to replicate those experiences – alas, my own spiritual career is littered with the empty husks of failed strategies for replicating 'peak' moments – but in order to imbue our whole lives with greater depth. It's in joining up moments of depth like these that we begin to transform positively from the core outwards. Seeking out the conditions that give rise to this process forms the heart of Buddhist practice.

Because depth, as I've been describing it, arises in dependence upon particular conditions. We might consider these conditions under the headings of *context, content,* and *consideration.* What follows is something of my reflections on how these conditions came together on that retreat for me – and I believe this is a good example to show the necessary conditions for depth – but I intend it to prompt the kinds of reflection that you might bring to your own experiences and aspirations for greater depth. And this is all in service of our quests for depth in the cyberloka.

Before I do that I want to be clear that I do think there are opportunities for depth in the cyberloka. In many ways, this represents a U-turn in my thinking over the last few years. Given the experiences in my youth and then witnessing the explosion of 'gurus of the cyberloka', with their high-production value content and low-commitment teachings, hacks, and apps, I seriously questioned whether the cyberloka could offer anything beyond a smorgasbord of superficiality. Having seen how, during the lockdowns in the early 2020s, the cyberloka could in fact supply all manner of opportunities for spiritual depth – from lifelines for those struggling to collective discussions, thoughtful talks, and even meditation retreats – I'm much more of the opinion that the question is not *whether* the cyberloka can be a platform for the depth I'm describing, but *how* we can use it even more effectively. That's not to say it doesn't have its limitations – as indeed do face-to-face situations – but I believe at least some of these can be overcome with care.

Questions for reflection and discussion

When have you experienced depth? What was it like? What conditions gave rise to it?

(How) have you benefited (or not) from online sources of depth?

Creating a context for depth

Returning to my example, perhaps most tellingly it was a retreat context. We can break this down into its components. First, there was the location: where I was and my physical surroundings. I was on the edge of a quiet rural village in the UK. But more than that, I was in the shrine room of a retreat centre, which, as I mentioned, is beautifully adorned with images expressing many of the different qualities that make up the deepest possible experience: the mind of the Buddha. Candles flickered and illuminated the scene, the scent of incense wafted in from the courtyard outside, and I was surrounded by the men with whom I'd been sharing virtually every moment of my life over the previous week. Even the way we were arranged in the room – facing towards the central Buddha image, a larger-than-life golden statue – communicated the direction that we all wanted to move in.

We might sometimes be tempted to think that aesthetics is just a matter of taste – what you like, what you don't like. But this is to sell its effect way short: the sensory environment around us can make a huge difference to what we can experience. The more our sensory environment is beautiful and explicitly connected with the best in us, the more propitious it is to the arising of something more than the ordinary. Of course, Buddhism doesn't have a monopoly on this – go to a gothic cathedral or an Ottoman mosque and you'll discover something similar.

This is one way in which our normal cyberloka experiences can let us down. We might be 'in' the cyberloka in a manner of speaking – listening to a podcast or reading an article – but we're also somewhere physically too. And that will form the majority of our sensory experience, whether it's hearing the sounds of the conversations of other people at work, feeling the vibrations of the bus's engine, or noticing the smell of the person who's on the phone next to us. And that's not including the sensory environment of the cyberloka itself – with its plentiful options for what to view next and the handsome, happy figures beckoning us to click on their ads. I'll go more into how the cyberloka deliberately manipulates our attention later on, but sometimes the contrast could hardly be starker: while the sensory environment of the shrine room helps us to consciously focus our attention and energy towards what's most valuable, the sensory environment of the cyberloka more often than not leads in the opposite direction.

This may make us sceptical about the possibility of depth in the cyberloka – and in the past I've certainly believed that we best avoid it altogether and concentrate our spiritual efforts in places that have been designed to encourage depth. Living through the lockdowns of the early 2020s, though, I came to realize that this attitude fell short. It compartmentalized my life into some bits that were 'spiritual' and others that were not. During those times, where physical meetings were illegal, most of us fled to the cyberloka in order to find our spiritual inspiration. What many of us realized was that it is possible to apply the aesthetic principles at work in shrine rooms and retreat centres to our bedrooms and living spaces, albeit often on a more modest scale.

I'd been doing this intuitively on other occasions even before then: engaging in certain 'rituals' before watching movies or reading a book – setting up the room, dimming the lights, putting all my devices away and onto 'do not disturb', and getting a cup of tea, among other things. If I was listening to music I'd like to have my eyes closed and all the lights off, heightening the experience of the sounds. If I was reading poetry I might pronounce it aloud several times to enhance the sensory experience of the work. If I was studying canonical Buddhist literature I might light candles and incense on my shrine.

This was all a way of making the experience special – savouring it – as well as an act of respect or even reverence towards what I was encountering. Not that I was totally consistent in it, I must admit. Reflecting on it, I realize that when I don't treat whatever it is with this kind of respect, it's probably because I don't actually respect it. In some cases, that may be understandable – learning how to do a handstand press-up from YouTube isn't exactly haute couture. But if I find that I'm consistently doing this, it does raise the question of what I was actually expecting from it. In some cases, my actions betrayed that I wasn't taking what I was watching all that seriously. And the converse can be true too – by acting *as if* I'm taking something more seriously, it becomes weightier.

I realized that all this could apply to teachings 'in' the cyberloka. So on the introductory courses we ran at the Oxford Buddhist Centre during those times, we'd encourage the participants to turn off all the notifications on the device they were using, create a shrine, light some candles – even just tidy up the space a bit – so that their immediate physical surroundings were simpler, more beautiful, and more connected with their inspiration. Then, even if we weren't physically together, the fact that we had commonly beautified our sensory environments along these lines symbolized that togetherness. In some cases, we could even see the fruits of people's efforts on the screen. And it seemed to work: even small changes meant that this wasn't just another Zoom[16] call or browser tab; all this supported a deepening of their experience.

So much for the physical context. Returning to my retreat, there was what I was doing in the run-up too. The text I mentioned was read out towards the end of a ritual, the words of which evoked depth verbally through poetry and chanting – another collective activity, of course. This followed on from several days' worth of silent practice together. And the ritual reached the point where we recited a verse in which we made a verbal request for a teaching. In doing so, not only had we prepared the ground through our evocations in words, but we'd entered a state of receptivity.

Again, this can often contrast with our activities in the run-up to encountering the gurus of the cyberloka – really,

---

16 A video-conferencing application.

we could have been doing virtually anything: firing off an email, watching the rugby highlights, speaking to our spouse. What *does* precede that flick-of-the-wrist moment as we turn to our phones? And does it support us to engage with what we find? Because we can enter the cyberloka so immediately now (especially compared to my first expeditions to the local library), it's easy for one cyber-activity to slide into, and even overlap with, the next or many others at a time. *Buffer time* can be the antidote to this – going for a walk, having a shower, changing our clothes, or even just doing nothing can help to mark the transition to a mode in which depth is more of a possibility.

More generally, when circumstances permit, I love going to the cinema, the theatre, a concert, or a gallery – and I always try to go with others and make an event of it, having a meal beforehand and a chance to chat about it afterwards. If we're watching the performance of a play or a piece of music, I try to read up on it or listen to it in advance, particularly if it is something unfamiliar or perhaps a bit complex. For a long time, with things like Shakespeare and orchestral music, this kind of preparation was all that stood between me and a few hours of bored incomprehension. This is the truth that experiences are preceded by mind playing out. And the same applies to our online activities – when it's possible, preparation will enhance everything.

Then there are the people around us – in a retreat centre, they might have been in silence for days, enjoying states of more and more subtle awareness, stillness, and sensitivity to what's around them and everyone else. At the end of longer retreats the team sometimes issue a 'health warning', a reminder to the effect that everyone else – particularly on the roads – *hasn't* been on retreat. Sometimes it's only then that the atmosphere that we've built up becomes apparent.

The leader is a key person on such retreats – a single person who holds the whole event – giving the main teachings to the group, leading the practices, and steering the logistics. And they're very definitely on retreat with us – showing up at all the meditations, sitting by the fire in the evening, and sometimes staying up after hours to continue meditating.

Everyone on the retreat also has someone on the team to whom they go every night to review their meditation. On longer retreats we begin to build up a deepening relationship with this person as they get to see us at times of great joy or difficulty on our journey through the retreat. We can also get to know them a bit – their interest and kindliness at the very least – although the emphasis isn't typically on a mutual sharing. Sometimes they don't say very much at all. Sometimes the little they say really nails something for us: shedding light on any one-sidedness that might have crept into our efforts or bringing to mind a relevant story from their own experience that speaks directly to where we're at.

It's clear that the meditation reviewers and the leader of the retreat talk to one another – sometimes it reveals itself in an explicit reference like 'I'm hearing that for some people...' or, most often, it appears as a timely 'tweak' to the proceedings – drawing attention to the stillness that's descending in the shrine room or choosing just the right poem for the stage of the retreat.

What about the people around us in the cyberloka (insofar as there are people around us)? Leaving aside the other people on the bus (or wherever), who could be up to all sorts, mostly the other folks in the cyberloka appear to us as notifications of attempts to be in contact, or as text, audio, or video. The guru of the cyberloka is largely aloof, I-know-not-where physically, separated from us by a gulf of pixels, filters, and time. Really, we have no idea how wise they are, and so often our judgements on this can be misled by our *desire* for them to be wise, perhaps in the hope that the wiser they are, the less effort we'll have to put in. Sometimes the more 'other' they seem, the easier it is to engage in this 'pseudo-spiritual projection', as Sangharakshita calls it,[17] which can be inspiring at first but also tends to encourage the idea that the spiritual life is something that happens to other people.

But more than this, the guru of the cyberloka knows nothing of *us*: who we are, what our needs are. Broadcast teachings can only get us so far. Eventually we'll need to talk to more experienced people whom we know well enough to trust, and who know us well enough to offer us specific guidance. We need *spiritual friends*. The guru of the cyberloka doesn't offer friendship – how can he or she offer friendship to their 1.27 million subscribers? At best they offer generalized advice, which may or may not be relevant to us. Friendship – that warm, common concern for one another, and sharing of our lives – is such a key ingredient in the context for depth, apart from anything because those moments of depth don't necessarily occur during 'formal' sessions. So often, in fact, it's in the hanging out afterwards that things begin to deepen.

---

17 Sangharakshita, 'Enlightenment as experience and non-experience' (1975), available at https://www.freebuddhistaudio.com/audio/details?num=119, accessed on 7 February 2022.

The guru of the cyberloka apart, I have found that, in the right hands, the cyberloka does afford us plenty of opportunities for (spiritual and other) friendships to form. I've experienced this most vividly on a door-to-door fundraising appeal where the team gathered only on Zoom. I was one of three participants from different cities who met almost daily for training and checking in about our fundraising on the previous evening. Beforehand I knew one of the others a little, and the third member of the team only by their positive reputation. After a few weeks I felt that we were starting to gel, sharing quite intimate aspects of our lives, helping each other through tough patches, and enjoying some great banter. Of the things that supported our friendships to deepen, I suspect the fact that we met every day, were having intense experiences in parallel to one another, and were already strong communicators made a difference. That there were only three of us probably helped too. Frequency of contact, commonality of experience, and openness to communication are some of the main ingredients in getting to know other people in all circumstances, but for reasons we'll go into in Chapter 3 the cyberloka demands much more of us in these areas.

Finally, our internal states shape the context. On retreat, we're just more aware – in a broader and more embodied way. We're less likely to be caught in distractions, and we can stay with discomfort for longer before seeking distraction from it. We have more energy at our disposal. And we might feel more confident in ourselves and the possibility of depth. None of these is exclusive to retreat conditions, but to bring them into the cyberloka takes some practice. Screens can be very stimulating – they're designed to draw us in – and the internal conditions for depth demand a certain amount of stillness. So I don't think there's any substitute for time away from our screens, especially time devoted to mindfulness of the body.

So, in a way, the same conditions for depth hold whether we're physically in a retreat centre or in the cyberloka. The main difference is that a retreat centre takes care of a lot of these conditions for us. But identical principles apply. Whatever we're reading, watching, or listening to, if we want to experience it more deeply the context matters. The more simple, beautiful, and inspiring the physical and sensory conditions around us, the more our minds will be drawn towards the aesthetics of depth. We can prepare ourselves by doing things that quieten the mind and help us to feel receptive. We can be in contact with friends who are also seeking depth and with whom we can discuss whatever arises. And we can give ourselves time to tune into our bodily awareness. Unlike in a retreat centre, when we're in the cyberloka we have to set up these conditions for ourselves.

Questions for reflection and discussion

What are the contexts like in which you engage with online content – your physical surroundings, how you prepare, the people around you, and your own mental states?

Do you notice the difference between these contexts? Which are better or worse for experiencing depth?

How to choose content

The Buddha's advice

So much for context, what about content? The Buddha has lots to say about the kind of content that supports deepening. Take, for example, his advice to Meghiya:

> [T]alk that is effacing, a help in opening up the mind, and which conduces to complete turning away, dispassion, cessation, peace, direct knowledge, enlightenment, and Nibbana – that is, talk about fewness of wishes, talk about contentment, talk about seclusion, talk about being non-gregarious, talk about putting forth energy, talk about virtue, talk about concentration, talk about wisdom, talk about deliverance, talk about the knowledge and vision of deliverance. When mind-deliverance is as yet immature, Meghiya, this [...] leads to its maturity.[18]

How does this list strike you – maybe a bit on the lofty or pious side? As with any canonical text, this passage needs some interpretation. The way I see it, the Buddha gives Meghiya two suggestions for how to choose content that will lead him from superficiality to depth.

The first is to consider the *effect* on oneself. Does the content beef up our egos in some way, or does it give us sobering but helpful feedback? Does it intoxicate us, or does it bring us around to fresh ways of looking? Does it help to move us in the direction of the Buddha's experience – the quintessence of depth?

---

18 *The Udana and Itivuttaka: Two Classics of the Pali Canon*, trans. John D. Ireland, Buddhist Publication Society, Kandy 2007, p.49.

Then the Buddha suggests considering the *subject* – alighting on topics such as simplifying one's life, the spiritual path, and the fruits of treading that path. By considering both angles, he covers all the bases. Even if a topic is not explicitly mentioned in the list he gives, talk about it might nevertheless have a positive effect on us. It also suggests that the way we talk about something is a factor in whether it leads to depth – not just any old conflab about enlightenment will do.

I think this is really helpful as a rough-and-ready guide for the unenviable task of discerning what, among all the content available in the cyberloka, will lead us in the direction of depth. But we'll still probably want more of a steer than this.

Discerning depth in general
Over the years – mostly through making the mistakes I mentioned earlier – I've arrived at some general principles to help me sift through what I do and do not really want to engage with online. 'Sift' is probably putting it a bit lightly: it's more like ruthlessly discarding the 99.9 per cent dross to arrive at something that's actually worth spending my precious life looking at. See what you think of these ideas, and add to them your own.

Not willing to pay for it? Not worth it
As I say, I've accumulated large quantities of music that I've never listened to. I've also had some uninspiring encounters with video piracy. Reflecting on these experiences, I've arrived at a reliable decision-making procedure for gauging my interest in something: if I'm not prepared to pay the asking price, even if it's 'good', I'm probably not that interested. The

prices of streaming media online might strike me as excessive – and don't those fat-cat executives make enough money already? But I've found it helpful to separate these two lines of thought: the excesses of Hollywood are one thing (and relevant in many respects), but whether I'm actually 'into' what they're offering is another.

Over time I've realized that what I'm prepared to do with my money is a good indicator of what I'm into, what I value. And so, if I don't value something enough to part with cash over it, I'd probably be better off doing something else. The same goes for all media that I consume online – news, apps, games, whatever. This is, of course, in addition to the basic ethical principle of not taking the not-given, and my wider desire to support independent creatives. Paying for something can also begin to turn my mind towards appreciating it, rather than just acquiring it. The difference may be slight, but sometimes just knowing that I've committed to paying for something reminds me that it does have value, and I can dwell on this to enter into a more appreciative mindset towards it.

The test of time

Being part of a close-knit Buddhist community, even in the few years I've been a part of it, I've been witness to several waves of fads passing through: new books, new meditation techniques, new online personalities, new apps, new insights into current affairs, or some combination of all of the above. With some of these fads, I've been very much caught on the crest of the wave. Others I've clocked from a distance, and either swum ashore or joined only when its initial energy has dissipated. With the majority, I've just waited to see what comes of it – which makes me not exactly a 'resister', but perhaps more of a *laggard*. Not the sexiest label, I know, but this attitude can give me some perspective, especially in the face of hype. I'd like to aspire to a ten-year principle (although the number ten is probably more symbolic of a decent amount of time than to be taken literally): if something is still being talked about, used, developed, and respected after ten years, fine, I'll give it a go. In practice, though, it's rare for much enthusiasm to last beyond the first year, and often, once the hype's over, the evangelists just move on to the next thing. But what really does stand the test of time – books that people are still talking about after ten or more years, for example – now that's really something.

I came up with a parallel point after feeling the negative effects of a year or so of social media overconsumption. I'd got to the point where I was reflecting back over the year and the journey of my moods in relation to the now-deceased threads, and thought – what would I be like if I spent the next thirty years in this way? It wasn't a good look. The principle I alighted on was this: allocating time to the content in proportion to how long I expect it to remain in circulation.

I'll give you some examples. Little text boxes on Facebook? High-definition portraits of dinner on Instagram? Teen dancing on TikTok? A witty re-re-tweet from someone somewhere I've never heard of? If I can still find them even the next day, I'm doing well. For phenomena as ephemeral as this, I try to give them very little attention – in fact, by the time I've seen them (laggard that I am), virtually everyone, maybe even the poster, has forgotten about them. Great works of literature, music, art, film? If they've had a shelf life of a few hundred years already

– or look set to (which is not easy to know at the outset) – I'd like to give them plenty of time, love, attention, and they will give me oodles in return.

Adopting this principle virtually eliminated my more 'social' interactions on social media (work interactions notwithstanding), supported subsequent years of markedly better mental health, and even kindled a thoroughly undeserved reputation for being 'cultured'. Of course, it has made me ignorant of lots of things that other people are interested in – although, in my experience, no one's ever shy about sharing that sort of thing if I ask, and, so long as I can live with the stigma of being the last to find out something, the pay-off in other respects is totally worth it.

The testimony of the wise
I have some friends – those I consider wiser than myself – whom I regularly ask for recommendations on what to see or listen to. In one case, a friend even gave me a four-page reading list broken down into authors (all of whose books I should read), their best book to start with, my friend's personal favourite, and any our teacher recommended to him. This is invaluable.

One of the upsides of the cyberloka is that it is steeped in a horizontal worldview, which allows for a rich profusion and plurality of content from all sections of humanity – there's no authority dictating what can and cannot be posted (up to a point). But one of the downsides of the cyberloka is that *it is steeped in a horizontal worldview* – and, in fact, not everyone's content is equally good. That a particular video gets several billion views, for example, is no guarantee of quality.

There are people I know personally and respect whose recommendation really counts for something – in some cases, more than any conceivable number of 'likes'. With their recommendations, I know I'm in for a treat. Of course, no one is completely immune to passing fads, but if I find a number of trusted friends pointing towards a certain film or book or piece of music, from different angles and at different times, then I know that's worth a look.

The rest of my life

Last, I try to consider how what I engage with sits with the rest of my life. As my student experience of Blackwell's testifies, I'm not going to be able to watch, listen to, or read everything. Even when I've whittled down the field with the above principles, that still leaves *loads*. So an important question to ask is: what is my life actually about? How does this video fit in with the overall current of my life? This is, of course, a big question. To answer it, I already need to have at least a sense of what the current of my life is, but for a lot of us we're still very much in the process of working that out. Nevertheless, some things will resonate with other aspects of my life more than others – over time I have got better at knowing what inspires me. And then there's following those inspirations to their depths in the face of all the other distracting influences around us. The opposite – a life lived following clickbait – amounts to the most superficial engagement with the most superficial input.

Questions for reflection and discussion

What *is* your life about? What's important to you? If you find yourself returning to something again and again, what might that mean for you?

How do you choose what you view in the cyberloka?

How might you bring greater awareness into those choices so that you're more likely to encounter depth?

For your consideration

By 'consideration' I mean the ways in which we consider and reflect upon the content of what we've heard, read, or watched. The Buddhist tradition offers a threefold list of the process we go through to arrive at depth, known traditionally as the three levels of wisdom. These are normally translated as (1) the wisdom that comes through listening, (2) the wisdom that comes through reflecting, and (3) the wisdom that comes through contemplating or meditating. For an excellent treatment of these I refer you to Ratnaguna's book *The Art of Reflection.*[19]

Listening here really means 'understanding' – in the oral culture from which this teaching comes, the two are more or less synonymous. It's not enough simply to be in the same room while a video's playing, or run our eyes over a text, we

19 Ratnaguna, *The Art of Reflection*, Windhorse Publications, Cambridge 2010, pp.14–18.

have to have some understanding of the terms being used and how they relate to one another. So the wisdom that comes through listening amounts to simple comprehension of the teaching – understanding it on face value. This is an essential condition for any deeper levels of wisdom to arise.

With the wisdom that comes through *reflecting*, we turn over in our minds what we've understood and try to make it our own. We enquire into it so as to understand it more deeply in the context of our own experiences, as well as in the context in which it might have been delivered. We link it to things we already know and allow it to shed new light on old insights.

Finally, when we've made the teaching our own, we then apply it to our direct experience, often in *meditation*. Brought into a state of greater awareness and subtlety, the teaching is able to make its mark. Its relevance becomes clearer across the whole spectrum of our lives. Another way of putting it is that introducing a teaching into states of deeper meditation has the effect of transforming the way we perceive things, ourselves, and the world. It's like grafting the new teaching onto the 'DNA' of our perceptual faculties, meaning that we begin to see things afresh.

I want to draw out a couple of aspects of this teaching that are pertinent to the fact of hyperavailability, and then I'll conclude. First, this teaching presupposes that we're engaging with worthwhile content. Coming from an ancient Buddhist source, it assumes that the work of discernment has already happened – because the content is the word of the Buddha. For us it's not so straightforward: even if the content is 'the word of the Buddha' we at least need some assurance that the translation is reliable, as so much can go under the banner of '[fake] Buddha quotes'.[20] Generally, though, Buddhist canonical literature is a fairly safe bet. Branching out beyond this involves greater effort. But if the content doesn't have the potential for depth within it, once we've understood what it's about, there won't be very much for us to reflect or meditate upon. The process will just grind to a halt there. So this is where the test of time and the testimony of the wise come in.

Second, this teaching requires *time* to put into practice. The ancient assumption would be that one receives one's stanza, or koan, or pith teaching (depending on the tradition), and then goes away to digest, reflect, and meditate upon it. This isn't a quick job at all – it might be months before the spiritual aspirant goes back for another teaching. And it clearly is at odds with the way in which a lot of us relate to content, especially in the cyberloka. I notice how quickly *I* scan through texts on scrolling screens, sometimes not even finishing the paragraph I'm on before moving on to the next. But that doesn't support the processes whereby wisdom actually arises. More and more of more and more[21] means that at best we're accumulating ideas on the level of listening or understanding, but we'll miss out on deeper insights dawning.

So, in addition to discerning the content of, and creating the context around, the input we receive, we need time and space for that input to really hit home. This is arguably the most radical point in this chapter – *we need to consume less*

20 See Bodhipaksa, 'Fake Buddha quotes', available at https://fakebuddhaquotes.com/, accessed on 7 February 2022.
21 As opposed to 'more and more of less and less', a slogan of Sangharakshita's.

information and fewer teachings in order to master them to any depth. It's radical because this involves going completely against the grain of the cyberloka. And it's tough because, if you're anything like me, you will by now have built up some rather engrained habits around how you read, watch, and listen, and these habits will likely be going along merrily *with* the grain of the cyberloka. Probably to the point where 'normal' is basically a state of overstimulation. But the thrust of the teaching on the three levels of wisdom is clear: if we truly wish to transform our lives, we'll need to reduce our input drastically such that we're able to devote enough time to allow what we have already consumed to sink in. I can't see a way around this.

As with much in the cyberloka, this sets a very high bar for our personal responsibility. So long as our consumption of media is not visibly pathological, we won't be able to rely on anyone else to chivvy us in the direction of cutting down. The privacy of our digital lives means that only we can know for ourselves whether the way we are interacting with media means we're becoming wiser, or just distracting ourselves from the challenges in our lives or piling up more information about things. Not to say that information is a bad thing – and I certainly don't believe that hyperavailability is an intrinsically bad thing either – only that we're better off resisting the pull of proliferation if we want to move in the direction of depth. I'm afraid that non-resistance in this matter destines us to a life of superficiality.

But overcoming this will be a gradual process. I began my Buddhist life trying to read and listen to just about every bit of Buddhist media I could lay my mouse[22] on. And this was an important step in laying the foundations for what then followed. To put it in the language of the connoisseur, I was developing my palate. With a prod or two from some friends, I began to read beyond what I was naturally attracted to, in order to fill out the sketch of the Buddhist literary canon that was forming in my mind. The groundwork laid, ten or so years later, I'm reading much less on the whole. At the time of writing I'm concentrating on a couple of suttas from the *Sutta Nipata*, a collection of discourses said to be some of the earliest to have been written down. They're not long – a handful of verses really. I've been reading these out loud as part of my daily meditation practice for months now.

I'm also studying one of the suttas with a friend. We go very slowly indeed – on a good day as fast as half a verse per hour. If that sounds boring, nothing could be further from the truth. There is so much to be drawn out from these texts, so many relevant points for our lives, and so much to pursue in meditation.

If my case is anything to go by, as someone with a lively mind and an appetite for reading, this may be a common pattern. We'll start off developing a broad acquaintance with what's available, and then steadily home in on particular areas of interest. If we're Buddhist, we'll gravitate towards certain teachings or texts. We'll then subject these to the kind of consideration I mentioned above, making them our own and allowing them to serve as a basis for deeper and deeper insights to unfold. One of the joys of the Buddhist literary

---

22 A handheld peripheral device connected to a computer to aid navigating a graphical user interface.

canon is that it offers so many launching-off points for this kind of process. One of the joys of hyperavailability is that so much is readily accessible. The challenge for us, as denizens of the cyberloka, is to learn to discern, contextualize, and interact with the media on offer so that we draw out the depth that, ultimately, we long for.

Questions for reflection and discussion

Do you have your own ways of reflecting on what you encounter online?

How might you employ the three levels of wisdom in reflecting on your experience of the cyberloka in general?

What do you make of the idea of consuming 'less information and fewer teachings in order to master them to any depth'? What might that look like practically for you?

2

Sex in the cyberloka

Introduction

Walking along a dusty track in the heart of the Australian wilderness, you may encounter a pitiful sight. A discarded 'stubby' – a small beer bottle – is attracting a lot of attention from the males of the jewel beetle species. The stubby's appearance – smooth, brown, with regular dimples – is rather like that of the female jewel beetle. Only more so. In fact, so absorbed are the male jewel beetles in their romantic overtures that they lose all perspective. Gone is their interest in the female jewel beetles. Some of the males weaken, through lack of food, and are carried off by platoons of ants. Some remain in direct sunlight into the heat of the day, only to be baked alive. Observations of the male jewel beetle's odd behaviour earned Darryl Gwynne and David Rentz an Ig Nobel Prize in 2011.

Sad though it is to say, I feel a certain affinity with those male jewel beetles.

The phenomenon in question is what has come to be known as superstimulation. We all have natural predispositions to respond to particular stimuli. And being exposed to an exaggerated form of these stimuli provokes a stronger than usual response. For example, nesting birds would rather sit on artificial eggs than their own. And, in humans, junk food supplies doses of fat, sugar, and salt – all important parts of our diet – but in quantities far greater than we'd ever have encountered in our evolutionary history. In my case, though, the stimulus was porn: Internet pornography.

But it didn't start there. Probably I can trace it back to the innocent weekly events of *Top of the Pops* and *Baywatch* on TV. This was me as a small boy during the early 1990s. For most of my childhood, TV was the main source of images of more-attractive-than-average women and romance. Even as a preteen I found these images fascinating.

As a teenager, staying up post-watershed – that time when UK TV programmes seemed to take on a distinctly more 'adult' flavour – gave me exposure to such cultural highlights as *Tarrant on TV* and *Eurotrash*. These shows curated the weirdest and most explicit[23] content from TV around the world for the benefit of the British public. Getting a TV in my own room in my mid-teens heralded the start of an entirely new era as I could stay up as long as I wanted in order to watch, in clandestine fashion (through headphones and turning off the TV temporarily as my parents went past my room on the way to bed), the grainy Friday night softcore erotic thrillers on Channel 5.[24]

At around the same time I discovered Internet porn. At my high school, the library computer system was still in its infancy. These were the days *before* the comically overzealous URL[25] blockers that foiled innocuous enquiries into such UK places as 'Essex'. I remember one lunchtime, along with some friends, alighting on a porn site during a quiet patch in the

---

23 Which, by modern Internet standards, was pretty tame.
24 Channel 5, in the days of analogue TV, was notorious for its poor picture quality.
25 Uniform resource locator, a website's address.

library. These were images that were of a totally different order from the ones I'd encountered on the five channels of terrestrial TV. They were basically static images of explicit sexual acts, loading one tantalizing pixel block at a time (it was still dial-up Web 1.0). We were adolescent boys. And we were captivated. I don't remember how we got away with it, but we did, and I was primed to seek out those images at home.

But my relation to it was mixed. On the one hand, the images were very compelling – they drew me in. On the other, much as with my furtive watching of late-night TV, I felt a strong desire to conceal the fact. Thereafter, my forays into Internet porn took place largely when everyone else was out of the house, via an alternative Web browser, and were covered up by me scrupulously locating whatever files were deposited on our computer and deleting them. I must have been about fourteen or fifteen at the time.

Moving into my later teens, I started to go out with friends more. Following our abortive attempts at fraternizing with real-life young ladies in pubs (most of whom, we reflected later, were substantially older than us – like, probably *twice* as old as us), a friend of mine and I would retreat to his place where we'd watch *Television X* in his parents' front room. This became a kind of bonding activity between us: a few beers and some satellite TV porn rounding off another week. It even continued, albeit with some tactical alterations, after my friend managed to acquire an actual girlfriend. (We'd now forgo the more general fraternizing bit, but include in its place endurance-length sessions of *Gran Turismo*[26] during which his

---

26 A Sony Playstation racing game.

girlfriend would conveniently fall asleep, leaving us free to resume watching porn with chuffed impunity.)

Things changed again when I went to university. The administrator of my college's network gave off the air of concerning himself with *all* the activity on the network – I remember walking into his office and seeing the bank of monitors on his desk – and I was in no rush to disgrace myself by being caught downloading illicit material. So the practice of watching porn, irregular though it was at this time, tailed off – I was too busy making friends and falling in love to bother with it anyway – though the interest in it remained, latently.

That interest was reawakened when, in the third year of my degree, five of my friends and I moved into student digs in the vibrant Cowley Road area of Oxford and, more significantly, outside the domain of the draconian college network administrator. I recall coming home from playing badminton one evening and found all of my friends watching porn in our living room – the boyfriend of one of them had come over and was treating my housemates to a tour of favourites from his downloaded 'stash'. It hadn't really occurred to me that one might have a stash, much less that it might consist in such an abundance of *video* (and audio) content – evidently my perspective was still being influenced by my dial-up conditioning. I don't know how long afterwards it was, but this event must have prompted me to investigate what was available in this new world of broadband porn.

The answer, it turned out, was *a lot*. In fact, I found porn even where I didn't expect to. During my trips round the Internet one day I came across an ordinary video-upload site that, when its moderators were apparently either asleep or on their weekend break, played host to all manner of material. Which, seeking concealment as I did, was the perfect alibi, as it wouldn't even register a dodgy domain name on my computer, should anyone happen to look at my computer, which no one ever did, though I considered it better to be safe than sorry.

Discovering this new world had a considerable effect on me, far more than the infrequent and short-lived episodes I'd experienced previously. Much like the jewel beetle, my natural interest in sex was now hijacked by a superstimulus: a practically limitless supply of videos of other people having sex. Porn was no longer something I would occasionally partake in, when no one else was around, or as part of a lewd social atmosphere. With my own room, a laptop, a broadband connection, and freedom from any kind of prohibition on the content I could download, I was whisked away by it. Other students would take tea breaks, or cigarette breaks; I would take porn breaks. Some days I'd feel like I'd spent as much time watching porn as studying for my degree – and this was in the run-up to my final exams. I was hooked.

As well as my academic achievement, my mental health took a big dip at this point. Watching on such a regular basis these, let's say, rather-better-endowed-gentlemen-than-myself having noisy, athletic, and aggressive sex with inaccessibly attractive women took its toll. In fact, I doubt you could find a better way to make a young man feel miserable and inadequate if you *designed* it. I also found myself slipping so easily into fantasizing about the women I would see out and about, as if they were porn performers. And I experienced the gap between porn's impossibly high promises of pleasure and the emptiness and dissatisfaction that lingered afterwards. In watching so much porn, with its intensity of sensory stimulation, so much of the time, it was as though the rest of my life became deadened.

This continued for about six months. In fact, it continued until I moved back into college accommodation – back, that is, into the domain of the fastidious network administrator. At the time, I felt that it was to my discredit that it was only the fear of revelation that reined in my use of porn. Be that as it may, to no longer be viewing it was a blessing. Although the images continued to resurface in my mind, they did so with far less frequency, vividness, or compulsion. Before long, the fog began to lift and I found myself with more energy, clarity, and general good will. I imagine the same is true of overcoming any addiction – I don't have the experience to say for sure – but stopping watching porn felt like a liberation. As the impulse began to subside, I resolved never to watch Internet porn again.

* * *

So it's with some first-hand experience of the downsides of watching porn that I open up this discussion. In the meantime, I've reflected a lot on that experience, and increasingly through the lens of Buddhist teachings. Without in any way suggesting that Buddhism has the final word on porn, I do believe that some of its teachings bring clarity, the likes of which I've not seen anywhere else, to this edgy and, for many people, difficult topic. Unpacking this perspective will form the core of this chapter.

But before we move on to that, I want to add two caveats. First, I'm conscious that discussions around the ethics of porn so often end up at cross purposes because their protagonists hold basically different views of what porn is. I'm not going to try to define it here, but suffice it to say that the world of porn is no monolith. A comparison with the food industry can be quite helpful.[27] Mostly, the paradigms used in discussing the ethics of porn constellate around the mainstream 'industrial' variety – typically intended for a crude heterosexual male audience. But to limit the discussion in this way is like talking about the ethics of food while only ever referring to Burger King. I've discovered over the years that, for virtually any statement we might make about porn, there will be hundreds of exceptions. Internet porn is a *multiverse* unto itself. So in the first place, I want to acknowledge the plethora of different approaches both in the production and in the use of porn: not all porn is as crass as the stereotype; not all porn users are addicts. And yet the stereotype is what most people understand by porn and so will be a common reference point in what follows.

Second, I'm writing as a heterosexual man who has suffered the painful consequences of watching a lot of porn. As such, I'm hardly an impartial authority on it. Our perspectives will always be limited in one way or another. But conversations around porn rapidly and reliably show up these limitations. While I'm aware that my account will certainly bear its own unintended biases, I also want to stress that I'm deliberately

---

27 See Mari Mikkola, *Pornography: A Philosophical Introduction*, Oxford University Press, Oxford 2019, for my inspiration for this comparison.

trying to counter a certain one-sidedness that I witness in some of these conversations. Often they focus, understandably, on the welfare of those producing porn and its effects on women and sexual norms in wider society. These are important issues, which also concern me. But in this chapter I want to draw attention mainly to its effects on the 'user', because this is where I have most experience. I've also found that once the conversation moves in the direction of the other-regarding aspect of porn, valuable though that is, the needs of its users tend to get lost, some of whom will be suffering too. So again, this chapter focuses mainly on the 'consumer' side of the cyberloka, though we'll start to move beyond this towards the end. As with everything in this guide, the purpose isn't to offer conclusive remarks but rather to model a Buddhist way of reflecting on these things. I invite you to adapt whatever you read to your individual circumstances.

Questions for reflection and discussion

Have you had experiences of superstimuli? If so, how did you (do you) cope with them?

What's your immediate response to the theme of Internet pornography? How might this help or hinder your conversations about it?

Have you ever talked to anyone else about pornography? If so, how did it go?

The Wheel of Life

Drawing of Wheel of Life by Aloka. © Aloka. Reprinted by permission of Aloka.

I've found it very helpful to use the Wheel of Life as a framework for talking about porn. Without going into all of the details of this fascinating symbol[28] of life in all its joys and messiness, it's worth making a few general remarks about the symbol as a whole and what it says about how our minds inform our experience – the most fundamental Buddhist teaching. We'll then see how this framework supports a more rounded conversation about porn.

First, the Wheel of Life is a symbol. Rather than describing things in a literal or analytic way, it suggests images that we can reflect on over time to reveal deeper layers of truth. It's the same for many Buddhist teachings – instead of giving us a definitive watertight metaphysical theory of reality, the Buddha invites us to explore how he came to see things, starting with symbols and eventually going beyond words and concepts altogether. Our theories will never be watertight and will require updating as we go more finely into a topic – symbols, by contrast, make room for a deepening exploration on their own terms. However, most of these symbols need at least some unpacking to get started with, so here are a few pointers on the Wheel of Life.

Obviously, the Wheel of Life is a *wheel*. And wheels spin – they go round and round and round. What this symbolizes is the repetitive and predictable nature of a way of life in which we unthinkingly follow our impulses. We go after pleasure, shrink away from pain or discomfort – maybe succeeding in the short term only to find ourselves back in the same

---

28 See Sangharakshita, *Eastern and Western Traditions* (*The Complete Works of Sangharakshita*, vol.13), Windhorse Publications, Cambridge 2019, pp.125ff.

position again before too long. This cycle is characteristic of what is sometimes called the *reactive* mind.[29] Living in this way, we lock ourselves more and more deeply into patterns of behaviour and thought that shape the world around us. Being stuck in these patterns makes us predictable and vulnerable to exploitation. It frustrates our natural desire to grow and enjoy more of what life has to offer. And it's boring.

The Wheel is constantly moving, without a final resting place or resolution, and so we move from a state of pain to another of relief and then back again or on to something else. Adopting this symbol to help understand our lives primes us to look out for the ways in which we reinforce our habits day after day, even decade after decade, and how this can propel us inexorably along the tracks of an underlived life.

The cyberloka in general checks out on this score on so many levels – clickbait might give us a dopaminergic hit, only to beget more clickbait; craving for 'likes' and 'hearts' in response to our posts only makes us more dependent upon them for affirmation. All the while, we're providing more data to the algorithms that feed us with the next irresistible recommendation. Which we then follow. Such will be familiar territory to most Internet users, and especially anyone who's had addiction issues with Internet porn.

The symbol of the Wheel also divides up into several doughnut-shaped sections with a core in the centre. Homing in on the second doughnut from the edge we see that this divides into six subsections, corresponding with the *six realms*: the long-lived gods, the titans, the animals, the hell

---

29 Sangharakshita, *The Essential Sangharakshita*, ed. Karen Stout (Vidyadevi), Wisdom Publications, Boston 2009, pp.179ff.

beings, the hungry ghosts, and the humans. Tibetan Buddhists understand these as our possible post-death destinations, this part of the Wheel offering a sort of travel brochure for the afterlife. If that works for you, great, but I'm not going to dwell on that interpretation much here. Rather, I'd like to draw out the significance of these realms for the kinds of experience we all will have in *this* life, here and now. We can see each one as representing broad ways in which the reactive mind plays out. See if you can recognize any of them in your personal experience (or in people you know).

The realm of the long-lived gods symbolizes the experience of immersion in self-centred subtle pleasure. Dwelling on feelings of exquisite and sustained bliss, we can fall into a false sense of security, losing track of the passage of time and forgetting that at some point it'll all end. Pleasurable though the god realm is, it doesn't last – and, for that reason, it's not the end goal of the Buddhist life. We can sometimes find ourselves in this realm on holiday if we're surrounded by beautiful scenery, clement weather, gorgeous people, and delicious food on demand. More traditionally, it arises from becoming intoxicated with deep meditations or higher aesthetic experiences that carry us away into an otherworldly, but somewhat alienated, state.

As for the titans, their realm symbolizes a strong desire for godlike bliss while going about it in all the wrong ways: declaring war on our enemies, seducing or dominating our sexual partners, finding any way we can to co-opt the bliss from those who have it. The titans' is a realm of control, competitiveness, polarization, and entrenched power dynamics between 'us' and 'them'. We enter into it whenever we focus too much on a goal as an end in itself and not enough on the inner transformation we need to be able to fully enjoy it.

The animal realm has no such goal. It's a way of being that sees nothing beyond the ordinary exigencies of food, sleep, and sex. Sometimes we want to just blob out and forget about everything else, dull our imaginations, and just follow the instincts of the body. Fair enough, we might say, nothing wrong with that from time to time, but it's also a realm of fear: with limited horizons come limited options when things take a turn for the worse.

It doesn't get much worse than the experience of the hell beings. Hell might not sound like a very Buddhist idea but, in a way, we enter it whenever our anger, resentment, fury, despair, bodily pain, or frustration gets the better of us. And reacting to any of these with more of the same only serves to deepen our torment. But it's not a matter of eternal damnation – our experience of hell, from a Buddhist perspective, can only be sustained so long as we continue to react in 'hellish' ways. Eventually, the reaction subsiding, we move on to another kind of experience.

The hungry ghosts, at least on the face of it, are probably the least familiar-looking of the denizens of the Wheel, with their tiny mouths and huge bellies. Theirs is the realm of neurotic cravings and addictions. We wind up in this realm when we attach to things like on-demand video, sex, food, and drugs a role that they cannot fulfil – as substitutes for connection, love, inspiration, friendship, meaningful work. Pursuing these addictions further and further, we enter into diminishing returns, the result being that those things fulfil us less and less and estrange us even more from our real needs.

In the sixth – the human – realm, we experience a comparative balance of pleasure and pain, of gain and loss, of actions and their consequences. In the human realm we have access to society, culture, science, work, school, family, friendship, and the spiritual traditions of the world. For Buddhists, life in the human realm is considered very auspicious – even more so than that of the long-lived gods – because we're able to stand back from our immediate experience, reflect on the kind of life that we want to live, and do something about it. In this respect, being a human is considered a position of considerable privilege. It's hard-won by emancipating ourselves from the reactive extremes of the other realms. That said, there are clearly reactive cycles that we will go through even in this realm as we navigate the ups and downs of life.

Lastly, as far as our unpacking of this symbol goes, each of the six realms of the Wheel contains the image of a figure, all of different colours bearing different objects. These objects stand for the antidotes to the limiting attitudes and behaviours of each realm. So for the long-lived gods a white figure carries a lute and plays a tune of impermanence, reminding them that their pleasure will not last forever and to prepare for its eventual end. For the titans, a green figure brandishes a flaming sword, not with violent intentions, but because this represents the incisiveness of a wisdom that cuts through polarization even at its most subtle levels. To the animals a blue figure offers a book, as a symbol of the culture and learning that can elevate us beyond our basest concerns. For the benefit of the hell beings a smoke-coloured figure provides a soothing balm of nectar to give them at least some temporary respite from their pain.

Among the hungry ghosts a red figure offers food and drink that will actually nourish them, that responds to their objective needs. And, finally, in the human realm a yellow figure appears as a sadhu, a spiritual wanderer, who indicates that the best way to make use of a human life is to develop one's mind beyond reactivity altogether. In each of the realms, then, the figure symbolizes the possibility of freedom from the limitations of that realm – we'll come back to this.

So much for the realms, their cyclical logics, and their antidotes. What might this tell us about a Buddhist approach to porn? I offer this framework as, I hope, a refreshingly non-moralistic guide to the many different ways in which porn can manifest in our digital lives.

Long-lived gods

However, porn doesn't manifest much in the lives of the long-lived gods. In my own experience of higher and more expansive states of mind, particularly those arising from deep meditation or becoming absorbed in beautiful natural environments, I've had little, if any, interest in sex or porn. Part of the character of these kinds of experience is a contentment, even a positive *containment*, insofar as one's enjoyment is wholly contained within one's immediate experience. There's no sense of separation between the enjoyer, the feeling of enjoyment, and what is being enjoyed. There's no need to reach out after something else. The polarization of desire, of which sexual desire is perhaps the classic example, simply isn't present. If we watch porn in this state, we'll most likely feel jarred and grossed out. From this point of view there's nothing to be gained from porn at all, so why bother?

Related, though perhaps more important for our discussion, is what I call the 'pseudo-god': godlike-but-not-quite. This came into my story in the decade or so after I quit porn. I'd stopped watching it, basically by suppressing the urge, and after a while I no longer felt the need to go near it. I then started getting involved with Buddhists and doing more meditation and going on retreats. I wanted to fit in, and so I deliberately gave priority to my more refined, 'spiritual' side. I wasn't trying consciously to deceive anyone; if anything, I believed the refined self-image I was building up. The term 'pseudo-god' seems to apply, because on the face of it my life was fairly godlike. I was in good health, good spirits, and I wasn't entertaining 'baser' pursuits. I was ticking all the boxes of the ethics of restraint. I was being a 'good Buddhist'. And, although in retrospect I can see its limitations, it gave me such a solid foundation in friendship, culture, and meditation that I wouldn't undo this phase. I'd stopped watching porn, and life was better.

But I started to notice I had a subtle contempt towards people who still did watch porn. I felt superior to them – even pitied them. Over time this began to suggest that something was missing in my approach. It suggested that I hadn't fully made my peace with porn. Yes, I'd overcome my earlier compulsive tendencies and was able to experience a brighter, freer mind in general – and this was a definite positive – but my approach was revealing itself to be one-sided. This contempt reflected back to me that I was putting a lid on my desire to watch porn from a place of aversion. It betrayed that, on some level, my 'ethical behaviour' was motivated by fear or hatred or rejection, possibly of my sexual desires – possibly of my weakness in the face of those desires – rather than a kinder, more rounded, understanding of the conditions that might give rise to them.

We're not, in this section, going to be able to go into all of the subtle distinctions between healthy and unhealthy ways to relate to desire. In broad terms, though, suppression and godlike containment can look similar enough from the outside – at least both mean we don't watch porn. And I don't want to suggest that suppression of unhelpful desire is inherently bad: in the short term it can be a necessary step in moving towards better pleasure (which we'll come onto), and highly effective when the desire is relatively weak. But, in the longer term, the 'energy' of the desire that's being suppressed – especially if it's being suppressed by aversion – will often come out sideways in contempt or moralizing, or simply stagnate. None of which is all that godlike. What leads in the direction of godlike containment is bringing these energies more fully into our awareness – feeling their manifestations in the body; familiarizing ourselves with their cycles; normalizing them as features of human life; and finding more skilful ways to channel them.

What it might mean to channel energy more skilfully may also need some finessing. Energy itself, from a Buddhist perspective, is neutral – and absolutely necessary if we're to move closer towards the kind of contentment the Buddha experienced. Desires, however, can be helpful or unhelpful, leading to an expansion and enriching, or contraction and impoverishing, of our lives. On a subtle level, in meditation we can learn to discriminate between helpful and unhelpful desires: preventing and eradicating the unhelpful, and cultivating and maintaining the helpful.[30] More crudely, though, it may be a matter of simply letting off steam in a way that doesn't harm ourselves or others. Here, though, we need to be on the watch for falling into better-but-still-bad habits – regularly needing to let off steam suggests there's still more work to be done.

In the longer term, both within meditation and in ordinary life, we seek to integrate these energies, so that they're available to flow naturally into whatever it is we want to do. This state of flow is just another way of talking about the god realm proper.

But I'll be the first to confess that I'm not there yet. In the intervening years, as well as within meditation, I've been trying to re-engage, often clunkily, with my cruder testosteronic energies outside of meditation: through martial arts, vigorous exercise, and working with the breath. These are things that, it turns out, I enjoy a lot, though they wouldn't have made it into my life under the previous regime. I have a strong desire to be physically active, and giving that desire a home means that it doesn't then 'compete' with other aspects of my life – such as meditation and reflection – that are also important to me, but require a subtler mind.

I've also experimented, from time to time, with watching porn. When the self-imposed prohibition appeared to be the cause of my contempt, lifting the prohibition inevitably offered itself as a way to overcome that contempt. If only

---

30 The 'four right efforts'; see Sangharakshita, *A Survey of Buddhism, The Buddha's Noble Eightfold Path* (*The Complete Works of Sangharakshita*, vol.1), Windhorse Publications, Cambridge 2018, pp.552ff.

things were that simple! The truth is, with a superstimulus like porn, there remains enormous scope for kidding myself that I'm doing something 'for my spiritual development', when actually I'm just getting carried away. And I have got carried away at times.

The issue, I'm coming to see, is not so much with allowing or not allowing myself to watch porn as with the way I was enforcing the prohibition: motivated by fear, shame, aversion, and rejection of my natural energies, it was unsustainable. Decoupling these negative emotions from my attitude to porn, however, *is* the way forward. I don't need to despise myself or porn to stop watching it. Rather, I need more awareness, forgiveness, and kindness towards the powerful forces that are at play in this dynamic, not least in my own psychophysical make-up.[31] I've found that friends can model this for me, even if I can't quite see it at times for myself.

But when I have been able to take full ownership of these forces, and begun to direct them towards what, at my best, I want to do with my life, I surprise myself with the results. I have a lot of energy at my disposal if I know how to access it, and when I do access it my life is more fulfilling. A satisfying, self-aware life lays the foundation for entry into the god realm, and freedom from the pull of porn. Pseudo-godlike refinement on the basis of aversion, however, is only

---

31 These forces seem to be almost entirely overlooked in contemporary discussions around gender, porn, and masculinity. I'd like to see a much more thoughtful Buddhist exploration of the features of male (and female) sexuality: an acknowledgement of the context in which it evolved, the spectrum within which those sorts of energies manifest, and the ways in which they can be transformed.

likely to keep porn at bay temporarily – and sometimes with negative side effects. Recognizing this difference has been a key part of my maturing attitude to porn, and sexual desire more generally.

Titans

If the god realm stands for a contented abstention from porn, at the opposite extreme are the titans, where porn's crude physicality becomes the standard for good sex. The realm of the titans, in fact, parallels the sexual norms found in mainstream porn quite faithfully: a clear sexual dimorphism, with muscular well-endowed men and petite nubile women, as well as a general mood of dominance, seduction, and aggression. Approaching porn as if from the realm of the titans, then, would amount to sizing up one's own sex life against the depictions in the videos. But of course, these depictions are pure fantasy. Even adult performers themselves don't size up as such: many of the men have to take medication to artificially enhance their 'stamina', and many of the women undergo all sorts of cosmetic treatments and post-production airbrushing to look the way they do.

Journalist Jon Ronson gives an eye-opening example of this juxtaposition between fantasy and reality in a scene he observed while researching one of his audiobooks on the porn industry. He describes how one of the male performers on the set was having difficulty getting an erection. Even the fact of his female opposite number sitting naked in front of him wasn't doing the trick. It must have been quite a sight: he, the paragon of masculine sexual potency; she, the epitome of feminine seduction and allure. The solution? As telling as the problem. The guy whips out his smartphone and, having navigated to his favourite site, finds he's able to get aroused watching videos of ... the kind of acts he's about to perform. The lazarusian effect achieved, he's then able to continue shooting the scene.[32]

What the titans are looking for is satisfying sex, but the way they approach it is misguided. By looking to reproduce in their own sex lives the tropes they find in the fantastical world of porn, in fact they cut themselves off from the satisfaction that comes from play and discovery. The realm of the titans is therefore one of an alienated relationship to pleasure. Arguably a similar alienation takes place by virtue of watching other people having sex on a screen – it can abstract our awareness away from our own bodies, where we actually feel pleasure. I suspect this is one of the reasons why watching porn, at least for me, has often felt so disappointing: I've wanted to have a pleasurable bodily experience, but because my attention has been drawn away elsewhere I've somehow missed it.

Hungry ghosts

Arguably the most unhelpful relationship with porn is that of the hungry ghost. Reading up on porn addiction in the process of writing this chapter, I'm conscious that many young men have had it worse than me in their difficulties with porn. Pornography has been blamed for,

---

32 The Guardian, 'Porn, sex and insecurity: How does XXX impact men? Modern masculinity', available at https://www.youtube.com/watch?time_continue=859&v=Tvsx-Y87HNw&feature=emb_logo, accessed on 7 February 2022.

among other things, a 'sharp rise in erectile dysfunction, delayed ejaculation, decreased sexual satisfaction, and diminished libido during partnered sex in men under 40'.[33] In the years since my own troubles with porn, various cyberloka organizations have documented the rise in these issues and sought to help people to overcome them.[34] The NoFap website and subreddit[35] is a prominent example of an attempt to help people (mainly, but not exclusively, young men) overcome their porn addictions through periods of abstinence from watching porn, masturbating, and orgasms (what's known in the business as PMO).[36] I can't speak from personal experience of these approaches, because they arrived on the scene after I'd given it up, but they certainly seem to have been very positive for some. By 'game-ifying' the process of weaning oneself off porn, they help people set targets and receive rewards through an app. Lively forums in which people can share their experiences also serve as veritable storehouses of common-

33 B.Y. Park *et al.*, 'Is Internet pornography causing sexual dysfunctions? A review with clinical reports', *Behavioral Sciences* 6:3 (2016), available at https://doi.org/10.3390/bs6030017, accessed on 7 February 2022.
34 Though other organizations have been helping people with sex-related addictions since before the advent of the cyberloka, Sex and Love Addicts Anonymous (SLAA) being a prime example of a 'Twelve Step, Twelve Tradition Fellowship based on the model pioneered by Alcoholics Anonymous'. See https://slaafws.org/8-core-documents/, accessed on 7 February 2022.
35 A subsidiary thread or category in the discussion website and app reddit.com.
36 Others, such as Remojo, a subscription meta-app, appear to take control of the user's devices and block all pornographic content, effectively enforcing a period of abstinence.

sense wisdom around the symptoms of addiction and what one can expect when attempting to let go of it. I can imagine all of this is supportive for people looking to overcome their porn habits.

What certainly doesn't help in this realm is rehearsing the arguments condemning porn from an other-regarding perspective (which we'll come onto later). The hungry ghosts use porn to satisfy a need that it can't satisfy – for connection, intimacy, energy, self-affirmation. Because porn is a superstimulus, like fat, sugar, and salt, we have a natural propensity to latch on to sources of it, and, if we're not careful, invest them with an emotional weight. This is why preaching to hungry ghosts about the horrors of the porn industry rarely helps them mend their ways. They're too emotionally invested in it to hear the other-regarding voices, and, even if they're convinced intellectually, a large part of them probably won't want to know. Successful approaches to helping people overcome their porn addictions must address the emotional need underlying it.

I remain to be convinced whether these cyberloka approaches ultimately do this. The process of 'rebooting' (to use the language of some of these programmes), when it is successful, helps the person concerned to arrive at a place where they are no longer reaching for porn as an antidote to loneliness or boredom or whatever the prompt for it may be. But the suggestion coming out of the Wheel of Life is that the hungry ghosts want something positive to fully meet their underlying emotional need. This is symbolized by the figure holding the food and drink that genuinely nourishes. In other words, liberation from the realm of the hungry ghosts isn't only a matter of abstinence.[37]

Animals and hell beings

I'll deal with the approaches to porn from the animal and the hell realms rather more summarily. From the animal realm – which is to do with animalistic elements in human psychology rather than non-human animals – an interest in porn is mostly just about following through on a desire for sex, and, once that's satisfied, it's on to the next thing: food or sleep, probably. Here porn isn't about anything else – in a way, nothing is about anything else in the animal realm. It just is-what-it-is without a wider horizon.

As for the hell realm, well, this account from an anonymous twenty-six-year-old man from Japan perhaps sums it up:

> [T]he problem is the more you watch the less it affects you and you watch more questionable stuff. My search for reality went for amateur porn often where the camera is hidden and the girl doesn't know she's being filmed. The other alternative was drunken party videos – often sorority or fraternity – because I was in a state of isolation

---

37 And, to be fair to these programmes, some do recognize the importance of positive antidotes – community, loving relationships, integrating our sexuality, and so on. And yet, for reasons we'll go on to in Chapter 3, I doubt these can be provided for within the cyberloka. But more than this, even these wholesome things, to be able to sustain their wholesomeness, need to be based in something deeper and more nourishing. SLAA recognizes something like this in its reference to a 'higher Power'. We'll come back to this before the end of the chapter.

and self-loathing such that professional porn seemed implausible. How could these sexy actresses ever lower their standards enough to settle for me? I know how this all sounds, these particular videos get worse and you often find videos where the girl is clearly too drunk to give consent. I hated myself every time, but I always went back.[38]

In the hell realm, one's pain and negativity find expression in a desire for footage that itself seems to depict pain or even abuse.[39] This is the cyberloka at its very worst – documenting, publicizing, and perhaps even giving rise to offline *violence*. I don't know how widespread the interest in this kind of footage is – it's probably extremely difficult to gauge anyway – but, if this is one's regular go-to, one needs to seek psychological and emotional help as a matter of urgency.

Questions for reflection and discussion

Do you watch porn? If so, from which, if any, of these five realms do you approach it?

How does this influence your experience of it? And what are the subsequent effects?

---

38 'Porn, sex and insecurity'.
39 Along with common practice, I would not describe this as pornography as such, but rather as footage documenting abuse.

Porn in the human realm

The human realm, you'll recall, is the realm of ordinary human interaction, free from the extremes of pleasure or pain, and giving rise to culture, education, work, and family life. I believe that pornography has a role here – just as ordinary real-world sex does.

I'm conscious, though, that a lot of the arguments about porn in the human realm seem to be guided by underlying views around sex in general – to do with its sacred purpose, its dirtiness, its capacity to exploit, its role as a vital part of self-expression, its appropriateness only in certain kinds of relationship and between certain kinds of people, its relation to mores around deviancy or obscenity in wider society, and so on.

For non-monastic[40] Buddhists, however, there's nothing particularly special – whether spiritual or deviant, ethical or not – about sex itself. It's not inherently *anything*. Buddhists do it in couples or groups, they do it alone, they do it promiscuously, they do it in committed relationships, they do it with people like them or people different from them, or they don't do it at all. But in and of itself it's just another part of human life. Sex comes into ethical discussions in Buddhism only when it is used as a vehicle for harming others or oneself – mainly through infidelity, non-consensual sex, and abuse of minors – otherwise there's not a lot to be said about it.

---

40 For celibate monks and nuns, sex, and therefore presumably porn, is prohibited.

Why watch porn?

Given the neutral position that the Buddhist tradition accords to many kinds of sex, I wonder whether the same could apply to some approaches to pornography. Without pretending to give a list of 'acceptable' ways of approaching porn from the human realm, it might serve our interests to give a few examples that perhaps don't get a lot of airing in discussions around porn.

Someone might watch porn to give them ideas to spice up their sex life in a long-term relationship. Another might watch porn because they're single or their partner or partners are not interested or able to have sex at that time. Someone else might watch porn as a way of seeking confirmation that their body type, gender, race, age, sexual orientation, sexual predilections, physical ability ... are not only ok, but that they can even be *sexy*, and sexy in a way they feel that they own rather than that is dictated to them.[41] People might watch porn to help them get aroused, where that might be difficult for them or their partner(s). They might watch it to relieve stress. Or they might just be curious. Or something else – probably no list could exhaust the possibilities. Just to underline this point: from a Buddhist perspective I don't think any of this is wrong in itself – Buddhism doesn't deal us a pre-emptive blanket prohibition on porn, though we need some sensitivity in looking at its possible harmful effects on ourselves and others.

---

41 Mikkola (*Pornography*, p.219) quotes Loree Erickson, a performer who uses a wheelchair, as saying: 'On a political level, it allowed me to make a movie that would not only offer a moment of recognition of how sexy queercrips could be, but also a way to tell others how I wanted to be seen.'

Does porn harm the user?

Well, from my own experience of using porn, especially when it started negatively affecting other areas of my life, on balance I'd probably say it does more harm than good. If we're able to remain within the human realm, fine, but given that we're talking about a superstimulus, this is a precarious position. How we relate to the treadmill effect, I think, is pivotal: over time, in order to have the same effect, we come to want more and more – and stronger and more extreme – varieties of porn. The limits of this tendency will not be set by the Internet, whose hyperavailability furnishes us with a practically unlimited source. Nor will they be set by social constraints, because we generally watch porn in private. So, as with our relationship to hyperavailability in Chapter 1, ultimately we have to define the limits ourselves. Slipping into the realms of the hungry ghosts and titans and hell beings and animals is a very real danger and not to be casually overlooked. Drawing on another analogy with fast food, a friend of mine says he relates to porn a bit like eating a greasy burger: fine to do infrequently as part of an otherwise balanced and healthy lifestyle, but not something to make into a habit. The art of the human realm is keeping things in balance, and if the user is able to do this with porn – without kidding themselves – good luck to them.

Does porn harm others?

This is perhaps a more involved and contentious area, and the direction the conversation goes in depends largely on what you mean by porn and which others you are talking about. As philosopher Mari Mikkola observes, 'it is hard to find empirical research that takes a genuinely dispassionate look at pornography's harms and benefits.'[42] Nevertheless, it is possible to indicate something of the scope of its likely effects on others: in its production, the consequences for partners of users, and wider trends in society. I do this to illuminate the range of possibilities we need to bear in mind when having these conversations rather than to draw firm conclusions.

Within this range, though, I feel confident in saying that a lot of porn *does* harm the people involved in producing it, for example by pressuring performers into undertaking acts that they are not comfortable with, financially exploiting them, or exposing them to sexually transmitted infections.[43] The very existence of institutions like the Adult Performer Advocate Committee and their wince-inducing, though 'safe for work',[44] 'Porn 101' advice to would-be performers bears all this out.[45]

The mental health of adult performers is also reported as an ongoing issue – both in the sense that the porn industry draws on a pool of people who often have prior psychological issues and/or a history of sexual abuse, and the question of whether work in the industry creates those issues in itself.[46] Directions of causality here are difficult to determine, and, as the average

---

42 Mikkola, *Pornography*, p.262.
43 And this is leaving aside the relationship between some porn production and sex trafficking.
44 'Safe for work' (SFW), a common Internet euphemism meaning 'doesn't contain material that will compromise your relationship with your boss if found viewing it at work'; contrasted with NSFW.
45 Adult Performer Advocate Committee, 'Porn 101', available at https://www.apac-usa.com/porn-101-video, accessed on 7 February 2022.
46 C.R. Grudzen *et al.*, 'Comparison of the mental health of female adult film performers and other young women in California', available at https://ps.psychiatryonline.org/doi/full/10.1176/ps.62.6.pss6206_0639, accessed on 7 February 2022.

career of a performer is around six to eighteen months,[47] there is a dearth of longitudinal studies. That said, this clearly raises questions around the effects of the porn industry on the people involved in acting in and producing it.

Then there are the effects of mainstream porn on the partners of users. For example, there seems to be some evidence that porn motivates acts of sexual violence. Again, overviews of studies in this area are unable to draw a conclusive causative relation between watching more aggressive or violent porn and perpetrating acts of violence.[48] Nevertheless, the claim gains support from the truth that what one dwells upon becomes the inclination of one's mind,[49] and that the inclination of one's mind tends to find expression in one's actions. Whether, in the cases of those who do act out sexual violence, porn merely amplifies an existing disposition, creates it, or is totally unrelated to it is difficult to say. Even in less extreme forms, it seems likely that porn influences what we view as acceptable – or even expectable – sexual behaviours. And that can't but affect the way in which we relate to one another during our physical encounters. More subtly still, from the perspective of one's partner, even them simply knowing that we watch porn might make them feel pressured, threatened, criticized, rejected, and cheated on.

Or not. I know men and women who seem relaxed about

47 Stephanie Pappas, 'The porn myth: uncovering the truth about sex stars', available at https://www.livescience.com/27428-truth-about-porn-stars.html, accessed on 7 February 2022.
48 See Mikkola, *Pornography*, chapter 2.
49 *Dvedhavitakka Sutta: Two Kinds of Thinking* (*Majjhima Nikaya*), trans. Thanissaro Bhikkhu, available at https://www.accesstoinsight.org/tipitaka/mn/mn.019.than.html, accessed on 7 February 2022.

their partners watching porn. As with everything in this discussion, it's tempting, but often futile, to generalize. I don't believe we can say categorically that porn harms the partners of users. Undoubtedly the pain of a partner's addiction – which is more the territory of the hungry ghosts, rather than the human realm – and the adverse effects of secrecy and deception are likely to harm a relationship. But, for porn in the human realm, everything depends on the individuals, their views around sex and porn, the varieties of porn they're watching, and the parameters of their relationship(s).

Perhaps a more revealing question would be whether we're able to distinguish between the one-way, fantastical licentiousness of mainstream porn and the sensitivities of partner-sex. I imagine that harm will mostly arise when we knowingly or unknowingly import porn's values into our own sex lives, assuming they clash with the needs and desires of the others involved. With the porosity of the cyber- and other lokas, though, this is worth giving some attention to.

Porn's values

Because porn does have values. Perhaps most famously under this heading lies the sexual objectification of women. While there's extensive philosophical debate over this issue,[50] to me it seems a no-brainer – obviously mainstream porn objectifies women (insofar as they're involved). In doing so it likely amplifies the already heightened body-consciousness that many women experience, as well as a feeling that they have to live up to the licentious 'ideal'.

---

50 See Mikkola, *Pornography*, chapter 5.

More interestingly, at least from my perspective, and much less commonly discussed, is whether porn objectifies *men*. Mainstream porn portrays men as largely silent, anonymous, faceless, stoical, mechanical bearers of large phalluses. As I mentioned in my own story, this affects men – particularly in the areas of performance expectation and body image. While the topic of the objectification element of porn is, as I say, a contentious area, at the very least I think there is a discussion to be had around the ways in which porn objectifies *everyone* involved. And it's likely that this will play out differently for men and women, and for different sexualities.

Nor is the objectification element of porn limited to our sexual encounters. Porn's tropes spread into many of society's norms, especially around how we present ourselves, and especially on social media. Whether it's in the images of pouting prepubescent girls, or the men who are all abs and arms, or the ever-sexy-and-available women, there's little doubt that porn's titanesque standards skew social media and our expectations in that direction. Given that most of these standards are attainable only by the genetically predestined (or subsequently engineered) few, and only while they're relatively young, it's not surprising that this can feed into worries around our self-image. Arguably, porn is only one of many factors in these examples of objectification – the sexualization of culture has a much broader and longer history than the cyberloka – but society's seeming acceptance of porn's authority over the domain of sex makes it a weighty player.

As an aside, for me one of the fascinations about porn has been the *subjective* experience of the performers. The intensity of desire and pleasure that is depicted, I've reflected, is one of the reasons I've found porn so captivating when I've been bored or my general experience has been quite dull. Admittedly, there's an element of objectification going on too. But, to put it bluntly, it's not even the same with the sound turned down. Let alone without *some* indication of the performers' subjective experience. Watching porn offers a kind of vicarious pleasure. But that presupposes that what's at issue is as much the effect the *performers' pleasure* has on the viewer as the effect of the shape of their bodies or the acts they're performing. This aspect is completely overlooked in the discussions around the 'objectification' critique of porn I've encountered.

Then there are the social values that mainstream industrial porn presents. They are overwhelmingly uniform. Male dominance and female submissiveness feature as the most familiar headlines. But what of other genders and sexualities? From my limited experience there are clear and inviolable lines of acceptability in 'heterosexual' porn when it comes to how men interact with other men (never) and how women interact with other women (fine as a starter but the heterosexual bit is the main course). As for other genders, well, this again is apparently inimical to mainstream tastes, except as a kind of fetish. What also of the ways ethnicities and genders intersect and relate to one another? I'm not going to trot off a list, but if you've been in this world you'll know what I mean when I say that some ethnicity and gender intersections are rendered practically asexual by their absence. In short, mainstream porn stipulates very rigid rules on what is and what is not considered acceptable in the arena of sex.

Now I don't want to suggest that any of mainstream porn's tropes are essentially problematic – if, to take a controversial example, some women find it a turn-on to be submissive in their sexual encounters with men, and they do so with full awareness and ownership of their actions, so be it. What's significant from the discussion of porn's effect on wider social values is the *predominance of particular forms* over others, and the way this is likely to influence norms of what good sex is. There's certainly a plurality of healthy ways to relate to sex, but where there's only a single sexual ideal, this is likely to undermine many people's sense of sexual self-worth and self-determination. As far as my understanding of the Buddhist ethics of sex goes, sexual orientation and tastes are morally neutral – they come with the territory of the human realm – so to privilege some and silence others is highly suspect.

Ethical porn?
The world of porn is, in fact, extremely diverse. There are a growing number of producers who seek to address precisely the issues of the previous section. Just as with the food industry, some producers are looking to subvert the dominant practices and norms underpinning the main-stream – to produce 'ethical porn'. The discussion around this follows just about every discussion around the ethics of consumer goods. And the upshot here, just as there, is that, although some producers are clearly trying to be ethical, it's impossible to be totally sure that anything we consume adheres to our desired ethical standards. This might justifiably mean we avoid it altogether.

However, assuming we are in the human realm and wish to continue watching porn – and I'm imagining that this will even include some Buddhists – we might wonder what principles to bear in mind. The three I suggest follow from the received wisdom around ethical consumption.

First, ask around. That might mean 'asking' a search engine, of course. There are various awards and meta-reviews of producers and sites that can give us a sense of who is trying to do things differently and better. This will narrow the field of candidates considerably.

Second, enquire into their values. Most producers intending to subvert mainstream norms will supply, in effect, a statement of what they're about. They may particularly tout the mental and physical well-being of their performers. They may be looking to present an alternative perspective from the 'white heterosexual male gaze' that apparently dominates the industry.[51] They may be exploring how to use the 'objectifying' element of porn to make a statement about the way in which they'd prefer to be 'objectified'.[52] They may be trying to bring more creativity and humour, and even aesthetic sensitivity and art, into their productions. If they don't explicitly state their values, though, that itself is a statement.

Finally, pay for it. As we saw in Chapter 1, I'd encourage anyone consuming online content to pay for it in some way, unless of course it's freely given. I think it's especially relevant in the case of porn. Smaller studios and producers who are bucking the currents of the mainstream are regularly undercut

---

51 Mikkola (*Pornography*, p.252) on 'feminist' pornography: 'the aim [is] to depict a less distorted view of female sexuality, and the view that promoting – ethically and aesthetically – better pornography can play a valuable educational role by correcting false, mainstream depictions of sexuality.'
52 For example, with Loree Erickson, quoted in Mikkola, *Pornography*, p.219.

by larger 'tube' sites that harvest their content and serve it up for free. Then, the super-hyperavailability of these upload sites means that any attempt to seek legal redress is rapidly nullified by anonymous uploads in other places. Aside from the ethics of not taking the not-given, if we are going to watch porn but are unhappy with the mainstream, supporting these other producers financially is the only way to go.

So when we're asking the question of whether porn harms others, all of these considerations need to be taken into account. For sure, a large proportion of Internet porn is *dreadful*, and in ways that plausibly spill in from, or out into, real-life harm. People approaching porn from the human realm would do well to discern this and act accordingly. And yet the bad stuff isn't everything by a long way. Our discussions around the other-regarding aspects of porn need to be alive to this variety.

Questions for reflection and discussion

How plausible do you find the idea that porn can have a valid role in the human realm? Why?

Would you add or remove any of the principles around finding 'ethical porn'?

What has this discussion revealed to you about Internet pornography? And what might it be missing?

So is this where the Buddhist treatment of porn ends? Is it just a matter of remaining in the human realm and being a good ethical consumer? Well, no. And here we can return to the two kinds of ethics – the ethics of restraint and the ethics of altruism – as appearing in the Arahant and the Bodhisattva Ideals.

Porn and the Arahant Ideal

You'll recall that the arahant is someone who hears the Buddha's teaching, puts it into practice, and liberates themselves from the Wheel of Life. Inherent within this Ideal, of course, is a critique of the Wheel. Life on the Wheel is defined after all by reactivity – falling into limited and repetitive patterns of mind and behaviour that just perpetuate themselves. That is, until you die, are reborn, and do it all over again. And the human realm is no different. Here, the swings to the poles of pain and pleasure aren't as extreme as in other realms. Maybe there's even a lot of good going on – paying our taxes, looking out for our neighbours, and bringing up our children well. In the human realm, we live more in harmony with the people around us and this feeds positively back into itself. But there are still the pushes and pulls of reactivity, and the other realms are never far away. And, perhaps more importantly, *there's more*. The human realm is fine (and certainly preferable to some of the other realms) but it, too, is limited.

This Ideal can be controversial because it can so easily be interpreted to mean that Buddhism has a low opinion of ordinary human life. That, in placing the emphasis on the *something more*, we somehow deny the value of the kinds of things that give pleasure and meaning to many of us: our work, our families, our hobbies. For some people, this places

Buddhism in the category of the idealistic, life-denying, misanthropic ideologies that, really, we thought we'd seen the back of at least a century ago. This characterization is tempting to adopt, and easy to find support for in translated texts, but is fundamentally wrong. The controversy, I think, stems from taking the word 'human' a bit too literally. All realms, in fact, can be inhabited by hard-working law-abiding citizens getting on with their lives. The 'human realm' is a *symbol*, and is distinctive in standing for a relative balance of pleasure and pain, a certain success in keeping things in proportion. In saying that there's something more than the human realm, the Arahant Ideal points to a life beyond merely balancing, moderating, and micromanaging the ups and downs of life (helpful though all this might be).

So we see the picture is more nuanced than Buddhism denying ordinary human pleasures. What the Arahant Ideal proposes, among other things, is *better pleasure*. Pleasure that's not so limited, not so vulnerable to circumstances outside our control, and not so bound up in predictable cycles of craving, gratification, and then more craving.

Returning to porn, now, even supposing we're ethically consuming porn in the human realm, this can't be the end of the story. Watching porn is, basically, a limited kind of pleasure. It's limited in its content: you don't have to have seen a lot of porn to know *all* the tropes, which just get recycled again and again. After a while it just gets *boring*. It's limited in respect of the mental states and behaviours that we cycle through with it: PMO, before too long, begetting more PMO, in NoFap parlance. It's limited as a predominantly self-oriented pleasure, as opposed to partner-sex, which does at least create opportunities for giving and enjoying others' pleasure. And it's limited when compared to the deeper pleasures of meditation and of letting go of habits altogether.

These latter kinds of pleasure are acquired tastes, let's say, but are far, far more satisfying in the long run than the pleasure of using porn. The Buddha pragmatically teaches[53] that it's not until we get a taste for these kinds of pleasures that we can fully let go of our former go-tos. Here the analogy of other kinds of acquired taste can fill out the picture a bit. I'm told that fine wine is a particularly exquisite pleasure – the different layers of taste coming through and caressing one's palate. But so long as I'm, say, scoffing Haribo every day – and revelling in the sugary, fizzy, in-your-face explosions of taste that come with that – I'm unlikely to be able to appreciate these subtler and more refined taste experiences.

And so it is with porn. Porn is ever so stimulating. The flip side of this is that it can dull the mind and body, and wear down grooves of dependency in our lives. But there are forms of delight that don't carry these side effects, and it is these that the Arahant Ideal invites us to experience for ourselves. The challenge, if we're habituated into the 'Haribo end' of the sensory spectrum, is to refine our palate, to ween ourselves off the kinds of pleasure that have undesirable side effects. This may take the form of periods of abstinence à la NoFap. But, in the longer run, it invites us to develop a taste for meditation, aesthetic beauty, connection with others, and creative work. It also enjoins us to notice the unsatisfactory

---

53 *Tapussa Sutta* (*Anguttara Nikaya*), trans. Thanissaro Bhikkhu, available at https://www.accesstoinsight.org/tipitaka/an/an09/an09.041.than.html, accessed on 7 February 2022.

and repetitive patterns that porn encourages in comparison with the kind of life we have the potential to be living. This is a process of integrating all our psycho-physical energies, rather than leaving some at the door – and for most people, I imagine, it's a fairly messy process. Backsliding and premature announcements of victory will almost certainly play their part. But I don't think that anything other than a positive, embodied, vision of the pleasure beyond porn will do.

Porn and the Bodhisattva Ideal

Here we move into the second of the two ethics of Buddhism, the 'ethics of altruism', a perspective deriving from the compassionate activity of the Buddha's life, which some of the later schools of Buddhism made their main focus. These Buddhists sought to emulate the Buddha's 'cosmic function' as one who discovers a path to enlightenment in a world where that path had been lost, and who then successfully communicates that path to others. This became known as the *Bodhisattva Ideal*, where the bodhisattva is a bit like a spiritual superhero who enters into all the realms in which people are trapped and helps them gain liberation. So, whereas the focus of the Arahant Ideal is on liberating ourselves, primarily from the human realm, the Bodhisattva Ideal broadens out to liberating all others from the suffering of whichever realms they're in.

The Wheel of Life symbolizes the role of the bodhisattva in the form of the figures bearing the beneficial objects.[54] The

---

54 Traditionally, the bodhisattva of compassion Avalokitesvara.

symbolism, I think, is perhaps deceptively profound: the bodhisattva is both *in* the realm and not *of* the realm. He[55] is intelligible to the beings in the realm – they recognize him and his objects as 'native' – and yet he's not subject to the reactivity of that realm; he always points to a bigger perspective, to something *beyond*. This is what makes the ethics of altruism uniquely challenging. It means understanding empathically the many different kinds of lives that people live – to be able to speak their language, understand their troubles, and walk among them – but also not being so caught up in the cyclic elements of those lives as to be unable to point them in the direction of freedom.

While bodhisattvas are committed to the emancipation of others, they're not able to do it unilaterally. Their aim isn't to liberate people on their behalf, as it were – that's just not possible. All the bodhisattva can do is support them to liberate themselves. This point is partly intended as an antidote to the presumption that *I* will save the day – in reality, we can at best indicate the way for others to follow. For some people that might sound defeatist, but it's realistic: that our own minds are central to shaping our experience is a universal truth. All the bodhisattva can do is to enter into the realm and offer the beings there something that might help them to emancipate *themselves*. They are able to make a connection and open up another way of living to those people. But those people also need to be at least minimally receptive to it.

A lack of receptivity was a stumbling block for me. There were people around whom I trusted in all other respects, but I

---

55 As depicted in the image above, though traditionally there are female and androgynous bodhisattvas too.

wasn't prepared to talk to them about my troubles with porn. I could muster some bawdy banter with my mates, but that was about it. Such were the multiple taboos around porn, and my own limitations in communication, that I found it impossible to talk about. For me, and I expect many people, the main taboo is the widely held view that watching porn makes you a misogynist. Then there's hesitancy in talking about one's solo sex life, one's weaknesses (though this is probably less of a thing in general now than it was when I was a student), and any acts that could possibly be construed as infidelity towards one's partner. There may well be more. Watching porn, for most people, is at least doubly private: taking place in the privacy of our screen time, and then being barred from respectable conversation.

Bodhisattva activity in the context of cyberloka porn means, first, being willing to break these taboos. I'm not suggesting that the bodhisattva needs to be fully acquainted with all the varieties of porn, or to have experience of addiction. I hope that what I've sketched in this chapter gives enough of the contours of the discussion to be able to talk helpfully about porn from a Buddhist perspective. It's more about normalizing porn, sex, and sexual desires – recognizing these as features of an ordinary human life. I want to be clear that these features of life are not intrinsically bad, but refract through the six realms into behaviours and attitudes that require a spectrum of different responses. A moralistic monoculture around porn helps no one.

Almost every time I talk with young men about their experiences of porn, the same thing happens. It's like a tidal wave of energy, long dammed up by these taboos, finally releases. Emotions, ideas, questions, laughter, all pour forth. They are so grateful to have found someone to talk to who's not going to verbally wrestle them to the floor for their 'deviant' behaviour and who will listen to their experiences. We need to create more spaces like this – probably for women[56] as much as men, though their needs will be different, I'm sure. So long as the taboos remain, and so long as the conversations, such as they are, come from a place of black-and-white moralizing based on a very narrow idea of pornography, the many issues around porn will remain. What I'm proposing in this chapter is a Buddhist attempt to clear the ground so that we can start to have sensible conversations about porn. Such is the foundation of a Buddhist response.

This kind of communication then allows the bodhisattva to show the way to *something more*, something better. The bodhisattva 'liberates beings from their realms' by making this *something more* relatable and attractive to the people they meet: embodying it, modelling how to arrive at it, and giving others a taste of it. It's a matter of moving people, on the basis of genuine enjoyment and their interests, rather than persuading them of the validity of abstract arguments.

In the case of the theme of this chapter, it might mean, for example, pointing people in the direction of *better kinds of porn* than the mainstream industrial variety – with higher production quality, artistry beyond the clichés, and where the performers are better treated. This might help liberate

---

56 Pornhub, '2021 year in review', available at https://www.pornhub.com/insights/yir-2021#Gender-Demographics, accessed on 7 February 2022 (also 'safe for work'). According to the formidably thorough stats on this website, 35 per cent of their viewers – more than one in three – were women.

someone from the animal realm: replacing cruder with more refined aesthetic experiences, and considering the lives of the other people involved, can begin to open up their horizons.

It might mean talking about the fact that there are *better kinds of sex* than porn. Many people I talk to seem to prefer solo- and partner-sex when fully embodied, playful, and imaginative, rather than stimulated by a screen. This may make a claim on the titans, who want the best sex around but rarely see how their adherence to porn's values might alienate them from it. That there might be better sex than porn presents the titans with the kind of positive challenge they can relate, and rise, to.

Then it might mean exemplifying the enjoyment of *better kinds of pleasure* than sex – the longer-lasting, deeper, more satisfying pleasures that come from friendship and connection, nature and culture, meditation and, ultimately, the stilling of craving. This may speak to people in the hungry ghost and human realms: the hungry ghosts want nourishing on deeper levels, which all of these provide; humans with spiritual aspirations may see the possibility of a path of progressively better kinds of pleasure which culminates in Buddhahood.

Both of these ethics suggest a nuanced understanding of pleasure. Pleasure, rather than being an on/off thing, admits of a range of possibilities and arises out of many different conditions.[57] Mathematicians might speak of the 'space' defined by different dimensions of pleasure. In discussing this we'll bring this chapter to a close.

---

57 I'll assume in this discussion, for simplicity's sake, that the sources of pleasure do not harm others.

Along one dimension of this space are the different *attitudes to pleasure*, from the point of view of the experiencer. The Wheel of Life suggests the following: refined intoxication, crass alienated projection, following our impulses, addiction, or stepping back and seeing how they sit within our responsibilities to ourselves, others, and society at large.[58] Our hedonic experience will persist for only as long as its corresponding mental attitude – which might be sweet relief to the hell beings, but a salutary reminder to the gods.

Along another dimension are the more *objective qualities of the source of our pleasure*, ranging from cruder, louder, quicker, and stickier forms of pleasure, which dull our minds and ensnare us in predictable ways, to subtler, quieter, longer-term, and freer forms of pleasure, which brighten our minds and leave us feeling refreshed and satisfied rather than sowing the seeds of future craving. Haribo and fine wine, vigorous sports and a clear conscience, masturbation and partner-sex, stimuli and superstimuli will all have their place. Pleasures arising from digital sources will occupy a range along this dimension, and porn a subrange within it.

These two dimensions will inform how the bodhisattva approaches their mission in many of the six realms. They'll probably see that mission more as a case of nudging people in the direction of genuine satisfaction, rather than allowing or forbidding any particular acts. Pleasure, as I've been suggesting, plays a crucial role in Buddhist practice – and

---

58 As a limiting case, even the hell beings have 'an attitude' to pleasure, namely to distance themselves from it through focusing on their pain.

life more generally. If it's not pleasurable, why do it? But recognizing that pleasure refers to a large space of possible experience, and that we can progress towards better kinds of it, means the bodhisattva can meet and empathize with people's experience and thereby know better how to help them.

Looking through canonical Buddhist texts, I'm struck by how much the Buddha emphasizes pleasure, and especially the kinds of pleasure that go beyond the sensory variety we've been discussing. The Buddha invites us to explore *non-sensory pleasure* too – the pleasures of deeper meditation and of freedom from any limited states of mind. From the perspective of these pleasures, the sensory variety – fleeting, unreliable, and largely outside our control – is always going to be a bit of a let-down. Note that this isn't a moralistic point; it's more like an appeal to the imagination, as if the Buddha is saying: 'If you thought that was good, you should try ... !' Mapping out the space of pleasure must therefore include this dimension as well. In fact, it's these kinds of pleasure – in their infinity, timelessness, and release from self-preoccupation – that may help us to understand the kind of satisfaction we're seeking in other kinds of pleasure.

Porn, then, isn't so much an evil as an artificially low ceiling on our possible pleasure. As such, the purpose of Buddhist reflections on porn isn't to condemn it, or vilify those who use it, but to understand the many diverse ways in which people relate to it, and keep lifting the ceiling.

Questions for reflection and discussion

How do you relate to the idea of life beyond the Wheel – the *something more*? Does it sound desirable or not? And what implications might that have for you?

What are the sources of 'higher' pleasure in your life, and how will you give them more attention?

What might you do to create a context in which to help others talk more easily about porn?

3

The *Facebook Sutta* (SN 21.13)[59]

THE SUTTA

Thus have I heard. At one time the Blessed One was staying in the Kosalan country along with a Twitter following of 500 million. Upon emerging from meditation, the Blessed One dressed himself in his robes and wandered among the wifi hotspots for his daily newsfeed. On his way back, while checking the Bhikkhu Sangha Facebook group and reading an exchange between two monks from Kosambi, a post occurred to him, never posted before:

'This is cyber-dukkha. This is the origin of cyber-dukkha. This is the cessation of cyber-dukkha. This is the path leading to the cessation of cyber-dukkha.'

He continued:

'What is cyber-dukkha? Alienation from the physical body is cyber-dukkha. Distraction is cyber-dukkha. Feeling Zoomed-out is cyber-dukkha. So is emotional contagion. So is ephemerality. So is literalism. So is speediness. So is meeting with criticism. So is being separated from affirmation. So are controversy, suspicion, and disputation. In short, the five aggregates of media-clinging are cyber-dukkha.

---

59 The origins of this sutta are shrouded in obscurity and controversy, with many editions of the Pali Canon omitting it altogether. In recent times, a scholarly consensus has emerged that this sutta is a 'later interpolation'. (In other words, I made it up.)

'What is the origin of cyber-dukkha? The craving that makes for online experience – accompanied by FOMO, relishing now here and now there – craving for stimulation, craving for affirmation, craving to forget.

'What is the cessation of cyber-dukkha? The remainderless logging off, renunciation of accounts, relinquishment of devices, release and letting go of that very craving.

'What is the path leading to the cessation of cyber-dukkha? Right understanding, right motivation, right restraint, right medium, right audience, right cognition, right critique, right recollection.

'And what is right understanding? Here a noble disciple understands the "logic" of social media, their opportunities, and their limitations.

'And what is right motivation? Here a noble disciple reflects: "Why am I going on social media anyway? What am I hoping to get from this?"

'And what is right restraint? Here a noble disciple refrains from broadcasting their own negativity and protects themselves from the effects of others' posts.

'And what is right medium? Here a noble disciple chooses the appropriate medium in which to post or respond, according to the nature of the message and the strengths and weaknesses of that medium.

'And what is right audience? Here a noble disciple reflects: "Who needs to see this?" and is considerate of their audience, both known and unknown, near and far, born and yet to be born.

'And what is right cognition? Here a noble disciple is aware of the biases that undermine rational judgement and takes conscious steps to mitigate the effects of these biases.

'And what is right critique? Here a noble disciple wishes others well and wants to support them in growing beyond their limitations.

On this basis, they reflect: "What is the best way to help them?" *and give critical feedback only where and when it is necessary and appropriate.*

'And what is right recollection? Here a noble disciple does not engage in the various kinds of pointless comments, that is, comments about kings, thieves, and ministers of state; comments about armies, dangers, and wars; comments about food, drink, garments, and beds; comments about garlands and scents; comments about relations, vehicles, villages, towns, cities, and countries; comments about women and men, and comments about heroes; street comments and comments by the well; comments about those departed in days gone by; rambling chitchat; comments about the world and about the sea; comments about becoming this or that. Rather, a noble disciple recollects the Dhamma and comments about cyber-dukkha, its origin, its cessation, and the path leading to its cessation.'

Within minutes, the Blessed One's post had received hundreds of thousands of views, tens of thousands of likes, loves, and anjali emojis,[60] *and thousands of bhikkhus thereupon entered the Live Stream.*

COMMENTARY

Introduction

The Buddha wasn't really on Facebook. I must confess to being a rather late arrival onto the world's biggest social media platform myself. Although I was aware of it through my friends as a student in the mid-2000s, I couldn't really

---

60 Anjali emoji: 🙏. Emojis include 'smileys' as well as other symbols to indicate, for example, the emotional tone of a message.

see the point of it, having already entered into a relationship. (Facebook's main appeal at the time, from what I could tell, was checking out potential romantic partners.) So it wasn't until I began coordinating a network of young Buddhists across Europe in my late twenties that I ventured onto social media at all – again, this probably introduces some bias into what I write.

In a way, social media have completed the arc of the digital revolution. If we think of consuming the bounty of data, in all its forms, on Web 1.0 as a kind of 'breathing in', then social media and its dramatic lowering of the barriers to content production are a 'breathing out'. Of course, it's not just social media but also the coalescing of high-end audio/ visual technology in our phones with high-speed mobile data networks – but social media mean that we can now do with a tap of our index finger what used to be possible only for those versed in 'code'. The upshot is that we've become *creators* as well as consumers.

This, to my mind, parallels a number of aspects of the sexual revolution of the second half of the twentieth century. Chiefly, in both cases, there has been a rapid increase in the freedom and scope of self-expression as well as a degree of naivety – and, at times, even *wilful* naivety – around the effects of exercising that freedom.

Our collective understanding, though, *has* matured. Even die-hard 'embracers' are aware of the downsides of social media, as well as their benefits. And living through times of lockdown, social media have provided essential ways for us to connect, support, console, and gladden one another. This chapter draws together some of this maturing understanding, and suggests how we might make the very best of these media without succumbing to their dark sides. This, as with all activity in the cyberloka, is perhaps easier to say than do.

I use an apocryphal discourse of the Buddha to approach this topic from a Buddhist perspective. I'm not the first Buddhist to have put words into the mouth of the Buddha as a teaching device.[61] Nor, as I discovered, am I even the first Buddhist to have imagined the Buddha delivering a discourse on the topic of Facebook.[62]

The sutta starts in a fairly standard way, barring some obvious anachronisms. But where it really gets going is when the Buddha reads an exchange between two monks in Kosambi. Buddhists familiar with the Pali Canon, the oldest existing record of the Buddha's teaching, will recall that the 'Quarrel at Kosambi' occupies a prominent place in early Buddhist history. Without going into the full story, two monks fall out over the interpretation of a relatively trivial monastic rule, and it escalates into a full-blown war of words between two whole factions of the Buddhist community. Even the Buddha's own attempts to mediate fail, so attached are the antagonists to the disagreement. It's only when the laypeople become disillusioned by the monks' behaviour and stop giving them food that they begin to mend their ways.

This story illustrates how the propensity for disharmony existed long before the cyberloka. Nonetheless, the structure of

---

61 See, for example, the phase of Buddhist history known as the Mahayana.
62 An alternative 'recension' can be found at https://bodhi-college. org/facebook-sutta-sn-57-1/, accessed on 8 February 2022.

the cyberloka, especially in its subrealm of social media, seems to lend itself to the rapid escalation of disharmony. It was witnessing such an episode in my own Buddhist community that prompted me to reflect in a more sustained way about a Buddhist approach to digital life. Difficulties seem to amplify themselves most in text-based communication, and this will be my focus, even though I do address other facets of social media along the way.

In the *Facebook Sutta*, the Buddha then broadens out to consider the nature of cyber-dukkha,[63] its causes, its cessation, and the path leading to its cessation. This much is characteristic of the Buddha's understanding of many phenomena – applying the fourfold approach to offer, as Sangharakshita calls it, 'an insight into the spirit of the general formula of conditionality'.[64] Attempting to understand the unsatisfactoriness of the realm of social media is therefore a characteristically Buddhist way to investigate it further. This forms the first section of this chapter. The origin of this cyber-dukkha then becomes clearer as we consider our motivations for entering into social media – after all, we are looking at how our minds condition our experience, as well as the 'objective' situation. The remaining sections of this chapter then deal with the path leading to the cessation of cyber-dukkha, with a special emphasis on how we might best communicate on social media.

---

63 Another neologism, combining *cyber* and *dukkha* (from the Pali, meaning 'unsatisfactoriness, suffering, dis-ease'). Put the two together and we have the experience of when things go wrong for us on social media.
64 Sangharakshita, *A Survey of Buddhism, The Buddha's Noble Eightfold Path*, p.145.

Entering the cyberloka 2.0

Right understanding

'And what is right understanding? Here a noble disciple understands the "logic" of social media, their opportunities, and their limitations.'

As we've seen, the logic of a realm is as much a matter of the states of mind we bring to it as the situation 'out there'. But in this section, I want to give some space to the topic of the more objective situation. We'll pick up how our minds contribute to it in due course.

Freedom of communication like never before
Social media make possible much that was simply inconceivable in the 1980s or earlier. They offer platforms for communication that are in principle open to all – everyone can have their say and everyone can learn from anyone else. This democratizes access to huge amounts of information. And it increases the extent of freedom of personal expression beyond anything in human history. It's also highly attractive because it circumvents the control exercised by traditional media and purveyors of knowledge. We don't need to swing a job in a media organization to have a voice. Nor do we need to be members of elite educational establishments to have access to cutting-edge research and ideas.

The anonymity and distance afforded by these platforms also make it possible to say things that might, in other circumstances, be difficult to say. An extreme example of this would be whistleblowing, where an individual publicly discloses acts of wrongdoing by an organization or another individual. In the right hands, this is such a boon to those wishing to create a culture of accountability.

Social media also aid socializing, giving people previously unparalleled opportunities to stay in touch with one another regardless of distance. For many months in the early 2020s it was the breadth and reliability of social media that meant we could connect with one another despite being required to stay in our homes. The significance of this is not to be understated – lockdowns without this support would have been an altogether worse scenario.

But outside of lockdowns, social media help us to meet up with others close by. Indeed, developmental psychologist Susan Pinker points to research suggesting that for teens with expansive social circles, online communication *increases* face-to-face interactions: 'When one type of contact rises the other rises in tandem. In other words, wireless communication exaggerates the extroversion of outgoing, well-adjusted teens: the socially rich get richer.'[65] And a study on the emotional effects of social media on teens by the Pew Research Center found, among other things:

> By relatively large margins, teens indicate that social media makes them feel included rather than excluded (71% vs. 25%), confident rather than insecure (69% vs. 26%), authentic rather than fake (64% vs. 33%) and outgoing rather than reserved (61% vs. 34%).[66]

65 Susan Pinker, *The Village Effect*, Atlantic, London 2014, p.193.
66 Monica Anderson and Jingjing Jiang, 'Teens and their experiences on social media' (2018), available at https://www.pewresearch.org/Internet/2018/11/28/teens-and-their-experiences-on-social-media/, accessed on 8 February 2022.

This isn't the whole story, but it does show that there are clear social and emotional benefits, at least to some, of being active on social media.

Moreover, social media make possible the creation and broadcasting of content on an unprecedented scale. Playing slightly on the word 'media', we might say that this capacity to broadcast is distinctive in being *im*mediate in some ways, and highly mediat*ed* in others.

Immediacy in time and space

On the one hand, social media grant us immediacy in the sense that we can broadcast almost instantly, across vast distances, and to large numbers of people. To some extent this had been present before, but to nowhere near this degree. For instance, when I was growing up in the early 1990s, if I wanted to say anything to more than a handful of people in real time, I needed to either gather them in the same room or somehow get on TV or the radio. And even if I did get on TV or the radio, if my desired audience didn't see it, listen to it, or VHS record it, or they were outside of the range of the broadcast tower, too bad. Maybe they'd catch a rerun sometime?[67]

Now, however, I can – and occasionally do – produce live videos that instantly reach hundreds of people across the world, and all I need is my mobile phone and a decent signal. All this has happened since the mid-2000s, and it creates opportunities for sharing our lives, our ideas, and our ideals like never before. Used well, in this way the cyberloka has the capacity to multiply anyone's efforts to share something that

---

67 Not that I had anything of value to broadcast anyway – perhaps it was just as well the media were so limited in those days.

may help others. As someone committed to communicating the Buddha's teaching, I cannot ignore this.

Mediated by screens
On the other hand, the cyberloka is highly mediat*ed*. It consists, after all, of *media*. These are technological media in the sense of channels of communication. But they're also mediated in an aesthetic sense, mediated, that is, by surfaces – screens. At both ends, three-dimensional, felt, lived experiences reduce down to pixels arranged in the form of text, emojis, gifs,[68] photos, and audio/video content. This is potentially quite a reduction, as a lot of communication eludes the literal content of what we're saying. Some studies of human communication claim that up to 90 per cent of communication is non-verbal,[69] for example.

Looking into this research, though, the findings are subtler and more relevant to the cyberloka than they might even seem at first glance. What they show is specific to a particular scenario, namely, when there's a mismatch between what someone says and their non-verbal behaviour. In such cases the non-verbals should be taken as more trustworthy indicators of their attitude and what they really mean. Non-verbals therefore help us to clarify what other people are saying when we're in doubt. This is especially pertinent to text-based discussion, which can sometimes be very ambiguous. Here, though, *there are few – and often no – non-verbal clues at all*. And even in video calls, there can be quite a range in the

---

68 A file format for storing digital images and short, looped animations.
69 See Albert Mehrabian, *Nonverbal Communication*, Aldine-Atherton, Chicago 1972.

availability of non-verbals, with hands and bodies often off camera and lag times in video and sound.

Psychologist Jeff Thompson groups these non-verbals into what he calls the 'Three Cs of Nonverbal Communication':[70] context, clusters, and congruence. *Context* includes the environment in which people are talking, the history between them, their assumptions about one another, their roles (e.g. boss and employee), and their shared framework of understanding and language. Non-verbal gestures should be taken in *clusters* rather than individually – someone's crossed arms could signal defensiveness, but if their teeth are chattering as well it's more likely that they are just cold. And *congruence* is to do with whether their words match the tone and speed of their voice, their eye contact, and other body language.

In the cyberloka, in settings where we often do not know the people involved well, if at all, and do not have access to the context, or the clusters of their gestures, or the congruence of their words with their behaviour, sometimes all we're left with is the literal meaning of the words they're using. And maybe an emoji or two. The mediated nature of the cyberloka denies us the 'checks and balances' that face-to-face interactions afford us in understanding the other person, either as a speaker or as the audience.

Mediated by text

As well as affecting our understanding of what someone else has written, text-based media also influence what it is – and is

---

70 Jeff Thompson, 'Is nonverbal communication a numbers game?' (2011), available at https://www.psychologytoday.com/us/blog/beyond-words/201109/is-nonverbal-communication-numbers-game, accessed on 8 February 2022.

not – possible for us to communicate to others. For example, with email, psychologist Daniel Goleman writes:

> In contrast to a phone call or talking in person, e-mail can be emotionally impoverished when it comes to nonverbal messages that add nuance and valence to our words. The typed words are denuded of the rich emotional context we convey in person or over the phone.[71]

This can make the cyberloka a realm of literalism: we tend to take things at face value, and, even with a lot of care, misunderstandings frequently arise. We can mitigate this to some extent with emojis and gifs, but even these are 'stock' – they often lack the subtlety to communicate the tone that we want.

The fact that social media are mediated in all these ways means, as I mentioned in relation to porn, that sometimes our physicality can drop out of the frame. If we're not careful, we can end up relating to our bodies as simply fancy smartphone holders. Or maybe not so fancy. 'Tech neck' and other repetitive strain injuries from the habitual postures we adopt can bring us a level of physical discomfort and dysfunction that would have been unknown to previous, more active generations. On top of this, social media can relocate our attention so far away from our bodies that we're more aware of our device's remaining battery life than how distorted our spines have become. The lessening of our physical awareness and the compression of our experience onto two-dimensional text

---

71 Daniel Goleman, 'E-mail is easy to write (and to misread)' (2007), available at https://www.nytimes.com/2007/10/07/jobs/07pre.html, accessed on 8 February 2022.

can also mean that our emotional states sneak up on us – and then it's only after an outburst that we see how this had been building for some time. To keep a cool head, we need to be aware of our emotions before they get to that stage, so we can simmer things down, maybe by taking a break. Here, noticing a rise in our heart rate, our breathing turning shallower, or our face becoming flushed can offer early-warning signs of a looming emotional reaction. Being aware of these things within the world of text-box dialogue depends largely on how aware we are of them at other times – setting up positive habits of bodily awareness offline, then, can make all the difference when we're online.

Gone in sixty seconds ... ?

Phenomena on social media are remarkably ephemeral too. Trends, memes,[72] discussion threads come into existence all of a sudden – and can capture the attention of seemingly everyone online – and then, sometimes just as quickly, are forgotten about or fall off the bottom of a newsfeed. Some social media platforms, beginning with Snapchat and migrating onto the 'Stories' features of Instagram and Facebook, trade off the ephemerality of these phenomena. Clearly, phenomena are transient anyway; the Buddha highlights that impermanence is a defining feature of existence. But it's curious to see that this is much more of a *thing* on social media – the fact of the ephemerality of these phenomena seems to create a sense of

---

72 '[A]n activity, concept, catchphrase, or piece of media that spreads, often as mimicry or for humorous purposes, from person to person via the Internet.' 'Internet meme', available at https://en.wikipedia.org/wiki/Internet_meme, accessed on 8 February 2022.

excitement, urgency, and anxiety about missing out in a way that we don't tend to see so much in other realms.

However, the fact that something has gone off the bottom of the newsfeed does not of course mean that it is gone for good. Far from it: every bit of data in the cyberloka is backed up and distributed across multiple locations so that it remains safe, searchable, and rediscoverable again and again.[73] This is a sobering thought when we reflect on what we've posted in the past, particularly for those who have grown up during the social media revolution – whereas in previous eras adolescent behaviour would be charitably forgotten as one entered adulthood, now it's recorded for posterity.

Then there's how we apprehend things in the cyberloka more generally. As I mentioned, I'm aware (and I imagine this is true of others) that I tend to read more quickly on a screen than I would on paper. I think this is related to the quantity of information that can appear on a screen, and especially the anticipatory dopamine effect of 'I wonder what comes next?' that scrolling down a newsfeed can engender.

The proliferative nature of social media enhances this, though – it's designed to be easy to share and respond to what we see: comments are commented upon, tweets are re-tweeted and re-re-tweeted. It's becoming more common, even in printed news media, to see comments on high-profile commentators' comments on other commentators' comments. And there is something so tantalizing about wanting to know what someone said about someone else and then to comment

---

73 Google Data Centers, 'Data and security', available at https://www.google.com/about/datacenters/inside/data-security/index.html, accessed on 8 February 2022.

on it ourselves – we have to engage rapidly with the unfolding commentary if we wish to keep up with its incredible volume. Among other pressures that I'll go into below, this exploits a natural *social* pressure – sometimes known as FOMO, or the Fear Of Missing Out. As a social species, we are compelled instinctively to want to know what other people are saying and doing, as well as to have our say. At the scale of social media this means, though, that the pace of posting and sharing increases, the volume of content increases, and the shelf life of any particular post diminishes.

'Distracted from distraction by distraction'

The cyberloka in its most basic form is attractive to the human sensory faculties – bright colours, moving and transforming images, and sound notifications all absorb our attention into screens. Social media take this to another level, though, in the way they deliberately exploit psychological insights to keep us in their spaces. It's now well documented that, prior to Facebook's initial public offering on the stock exchange, they took to developing tools to increase user engagement. Why they did this bears some reflection. Consider the question: who are Facebook's customers? If your answer to that question is 'me', I'm afraid you're likely to be disappointed. Yes, their stated purpose is to provide platforms for connection, but they don't charge their users for the privilege. And yet, somehow they make a *lot* of money. In fact, they make their billions of dollars from *advertisers*, to whom they, effectively, auction off our attention. The more they can hold our attention on their platform – even if this means flitting from one post to another – the greater their advertising revenues.

Facebook's early attempts to generate greater user engagement involved things like the option to tag people in photos and the 'like' button. They then moved on to the 'pull to refresh' facility (on touchscreen devices), which soon became ubiquitous. This latter applies the psychology of 'intermittent rewards', well known to the manufacturers of slot machines – as we never know quite when we'll be rewarded with another 'like' or notification, we keep 'pulling the lever'. Lastly, at least in this short list, there's the 'infinite scroll'. Ordinarily, when we reach the 'end' of something, it prompts us to make a choice: what to do now? Infinitely scrolling newsfeeds, employing similar psychology to that of labyrinthine, artificially lit, and air-conditioned casinos, reduce the occurrence of natural end points, which is why we can sometimes simply lose track of time when we're looking at them.

All of these tools are now augmented by algorithms that are so sophisticated that they glean from our past behaviour what content to push in our direction so as to maximize our engagement. They know, for example, when in the day is best to release new notifications; they'll even stagger our notifications over time to keep us returning. Some critics of social media – increasingly the Silicon Valley wunderkinder who invented some of these tools – describe the situation as being like a supercomputer aimed at your brain, with one aim: keeping you engaged.[74]

So social media are a subrealm of calculated distraction. And *that's* not including what's going on in the physical world around us – avoiding other people on the street, keeping an

---

74 'The social dilemma' (2020), available at https://www.thesocialdilemma.com/, accessed on 8 February 2022.

eye out for our boss, or putting the kids to bed. The overall effect of this is that social media put us under *cognitive strain*: because they habituate our minds to respond to this drip feed of tantalizing rewards, we end up being torn between their myriad offerings, and between these and the other demands on our attention.

An unhappy medium?

The tone of communication on social media often follows the fact of this strain. Even a cursory glance down an average comment thread will reveal that it's skewed towards negativity. As Daniel Kahneman writes:

> When you feel strained, you are more likely to be vigilant and suspicious, invest more effort in what you are doing, feel less comfortable, and make fewer errors, but you are also less intuitive and less creative than usual.[75]

This vigilance and suspicion can create an awkward disjoint between how our comments are intended and how they land with their recipients. Perhaps we've all had experiences of our jokes falling flat (or worse) over text. But even more generally, our positive comments are often received as more neutral by their readers, and our neutral comments as more negative.[76] This 'deflationary' effect perhaps stems from a cocktail of many of the aforementioned conditions along with so-called 'negativity bias', according to which negative stimuli are significantly more salient than positive stimuli of the same

---

75 Daniel Kahneman, *Thinking, Fast and Slow,* Penguin, London 2011, p.60.
76 Goleman, 'E-mail is easy to write (and to misread)'.

intensity. More on this in the sections on right cognition and right critique.

There are also ongoing questions among psychologists around the negative emotional effects of social media use, especially on children and young adults. Certainly, a number of studies have observed a positive correlation between social media use and teen depression and suicide, though the direction of causality seems to run both ways – in short, mental ill health can result in increased social media use, as well as vice versa.[77]

And then there's general emotional arousal. Tweeting, for example, raises one's pulse, makes one sweat, and enlarges one's pupils, all indicators of arousal or stress.[78] According to studies conducted by Twitter itself, relative to just browsing the Web, tweeting and re-tweeting enhance brain activity indicative of emotional arousal by 75 per cent. Simply reading one's feed increases emotional arousal by 65 per cent. Neuroscientist Tali Sharot describes Twitter as the 'amygdala of the Internet'[79] – this is another way of saying that social media can be a realm of *stress*.

---

77 Referred to in Carol Vidal *et al.*, 'Social media use and depression in adolescents: a scoping review', *International Review of Psychiatry* 32:3 (2020), pp.235–53, doi: 10.1080/09540261.2020.1720623, available at https://www.ncbi.nlm.nih.gov/pmc/articles/PMC7392374/, accessed on 8 February 2022.

78 Sharot, *The Influential Mind*, p.49.

79 Sharot, *The Influential Mind*, p.49. The amygdala is part of the brain involved in the production of cortisol, a hormone connected with stress.

A high bar

Aesthetics matter. Understanding a realm is as much about having a 'feel' for the environment as it is about knowing intellectually what characteristics it has. And the 'feel' of the environment is arguably as much a factor in how we think and act as the behaviour of those around us. This is one of the reasons why Buddhists don't hold meditation classes in Burger King: the aesthetics are at odds with the nature of the activity – there's a dissonance between the calm of meditation on the one hand, and strip lighting and reprocessed grease on the other. And I would contend that there's a similar dissonance between the characteristics of social media listed above and activities that require sustained attention, empathy, nuance, and a cool head.

To be clear, I'm not saying I'm above any of this. We're *all* vulnerable to the prevailing conditions on social media. Recognizing this requires some humility. We may find ourselves overreacting, misunderstanding others, perhaps coming to overhasty conclusions, perhaps being drawn into long periods of seemingly pointless distraction. Knowing that this is likely can help to some extent but grants us no immunity. For all the opportunities afforded by social media to spread helpful ideas and connect with others, and all our positive wishes, we also need to be aware that the terrain will not make it easy for us. These media have massive potential, but we shouldn't fool ourselves about how much self-awareness it demands to do well.

Questions for reflection and discussion

What is your general experience of social media?

Do the characteristics mentioned above ring true?

What might be other positives and negatives of the social media revolution in general? What might the effect of social media be on practising skilful communication?

Why am I here?

Right motivation

'And what is right motivation? Here a noble disciple reflects: "Why am I going on social media anyway?"'

Recalling the Tibetan Wheel of Life, we can more deeply understand a realm by getting to know the mental states of its inhabitants. We don't just fall into a realm – our volitions and interests propel us into it. We can also look at social media through the lens of our motivations for wanting to enter them. Here, again, I'm speaking mainly from my own experiences and what I observe in others.

First, though, I'm conscious that it doesn't often feel like I make a conscious decision to enter social media. This is in stark contrast to my first experiences of 'logging on' in my local library in the late 1990s. Even when, after considerable lobbying efforts on my part, my parents eventually acquiesced to the presence of the Internet in their home, I still needed to go to the room in the house where our family computer resided, start it up (which in itself took time enough to make a hot drink), and then wait for a minute or so as the dial-up modem emitted its reassuring 'tune',[80] the ending of which indicated that, yes, we were at last online. In those days, any interaction with the cyberloka was a very conscious decision indeed.

Nowadays, however, physical and cyber realities are increasingly porous to one another – only a vibration, a ping, a short factual question, or a push notification apart. Sometimes it's quite Pavlovian: the notification arrives and we barely think about whether or not to follow it up; the gap between stimulus and response can be *so* small. I'm even aware of how dated the expressions 'logging on' and 'going online' sound now – don't we just pick up our phones? All this raises alarm bells for me. It begins to suggest that our experience of social media is conditioned by a lack of awareness.

Actually, it's a bit more complicated than that for me. Most of my time on social media has related to my previous paid work – communicating with the young Buddhists in the Triratna Buddhist Community and publicizing events, for a start. With these aims in mind, the subrealm of social media can make the job of a coordinator so much easier. As I mentioned, these media are designed with publicity in mind, and it's possible to tailor adverts to exactly the kinds of people who might be interested. With Buddhist events, that audience is relatively niche, but the precision of the advertising tools that social media offer means that

---

80 Nostalgic cyberlokans, or curious newbies, can experience it here: 'Dial up sound (HD)', available at https://www.youtube.com/watch?v=GSRG0TqxLWc, accessed on 8 February 2022.

comparatively little is wasted in our efforts to put the word out. These media also make it very straightforward to get a sense of the big life events going on for my more far-flung friends, and to celebrate with them. This can simply be pro-social behaviour – we are naturally drawn to reciprocate when others contact us and to share in their joys.

But I also enter into social media habitually, and with less clarity, as I'm sure most of us do. Then the motivations, when I start to dig down into them, are a little less wholesome. Often, if I'm honest, it's because I'm feeling bored, lonely, tired, wired, speedy, or grumpy. In these situations, I'm often craving something to distract me from how I'm feeling, maybe some little affirmative pick-me-up in the form of a 'like' or a message from a friend. As the Buddha of the *Facebook Sutta* says, in relation to the origin of cyber-dukkha, we are so often drawn into social media by 'the craving that makes for online experience – accompanied by FOMO, relishing now here and now there – craving for stimulation, craving for affirmation, craving to forget'. This links in with the dopaminergic neurons mentioned in Chapter 1: every time we tap a link, receive a message of some sort, or even see a notification, we get a dopamine hit – part of the brain's reward system. And just as with gambling, social media give our brains a cheap, quick way to feel like they're being rewarded. We crave that reward, and it's addictive.[81] Add to this the fear of missing out, and we have a 'negative' pressure for remaining in the loop. And sometimes we just seek the oblivion of some kind of escape from whatever difficulties we're facing in our lives.

---

81 'Internet addiction disorder', available at https://en.wikipedia.org/wiki/Internet_addiction_disorder, accessed on 8 February 2022.

What complicates things further is that social media don't actually address many of the underlying reasons for our being there. Loneliness is addressed by, among other things, meaningful face-to-face friendships; tiredness is overcome by rest; wired-ness by reducing input and relaxing; speediness by slowing down; grumpiness by a whole host of nourishing things; and boredom, often, by just sitting it out. Craving only intensifies when we indulge it, and we can only ever *postpone* our fear of missing out by trying to keep abreast with every new development. Long-term resolutions to these states don't require social media. Most of them *can't* be resolved on social media. And social media, at least in some spaces, can make all of them worse.

These situations echo the logic of the realm of the hungry ghosts. I remember one of the times most recently when I was using my phone a lot, perhaps even too much: during the door-to-door fundraising appeal I mentioned in Chapter 1. Sometimes I'd be feeling very nervous and uncomfortable as I was heading over to the expensive north Oxford neighbourhood where I was knocking. And because my phone was on 'silent' mode, I'd be checking it every few minutes to see if something had come through on our team's chat group. It'd be the last thing I'd do once I'd gathered my stuff together and was about to set off to meet people on the doorstep. But it'd do nothing to ease my nerves. Either I hadn't received something – in which case I was just left to stew in my unpleasant feeling; or, if I had, I'd respond and then be waiting, with additional anxiety, for someone else to reply. This was a terrible way to prepare for connecting with people in what could be intense face-to-face interactions.

Psychologists offer a general guide to discerning the effects of acting on our cyber-motivations. Basically, if we're wanting social connection or trying to make ourselves feel better, entering the cyberloka can mean that our psychological well-being drops; if we're wanting to find out information or acquire goods, we may actually feel better.[82] It's also worth saying that, in practice, our motivations can be mixed and that one can turn ever so easily into the other.

We may have all sorts of motivations for engaging with social media – in the *Facebook Sutta* the Buddha simply exhorts us to be *honest about our motivations* and become skilled in knowing how best to address the underlying issues. This alone asks a lot of our self-awareness. If we approach social media consciously, and with a desire to increase the general quantum of positivity on them, we may be able to have a net beneficial effect. Sometimes we can just feel that we want to reach out to others to share something positive in our – or their – lives. Sometimes we might enter social media with the intention of prompting deeper kinds of connection with others. Again, I'm not going to issue a list of acceptable reasons for using social media but, if they're imbued with awareness, loving-kindness, sharing in others' successes, reaching out to others in difficulty, level-headedness, and a desire for the best in ourselves and others, it'll all be to the good. The key thing is that we're aware of what's motivating us, keeping up the positive initiative, and not being naive

---

82 E.B. Weiser, 'The functions of Internet use and their social and psychological consequences', *Cyberpsychology & behavior* 4:6 (2001), pp.723–43, available at https://doi.org/10.1089/109493101753376678, accessed on 8 February 2022. This clearly predates social media, but the findings still seem relevant.

about how the cyberloka might hijack all of this. Without being too heavy about it, if we don't take the initiative it *will* hijack our efforts. It's *designed* to.

But if our horizons expand to include other people, the stakes are even higher: as well as being aware of our own motivations, if we wish to benefit others we need to be sensitive to what's drawing them into the realm of social media – even if they aren't sensitive to it themselves. A lot of what, to me, seems like fruitless exchange comes from well-meaning people trying to correct the views (and even behaviour) of others, while missing the underlying reasons for why they're online in the first place. If someone's in a difficult place – low mood, frustrated, tired, bored at work, failing to address past unresolved conflict, or experiencing mental ill health – giving their views a point-by-point deconstruction in a public space is unlikely to be what they need. Adding something positive into the mix in these circumstances requires imagination and patience – more on this later.

These days I try to become more conscious of *when* and *why* I'm using my devices. I tend to wait until after breakfast to look at screens and avoid them after my evening meal. If I'm doing anything that involves sustained thinking – writing this book, for example – I'll switch off *all* my notifications on every device, have only one window open at a time (normally the word processor), and allow only very specific tabs to be open on my Web browser. I try to do the same even when I'm writing emails.

I'm also aware of, and attempt to counteract, the tendency to think 'I've got a couple of minutes before the next thing starts, I'll just check my ... ' – I can so easily fall into this grasping mindset, which social media only feed. Often the effect of indulging it is to have lots of unresolved 'stuff' going on in my mind as I enter into the next activity, which detracts from being able to give my full attention to the new situation.

A few years ago, I used to do a short ritual in the morning before switching on my devices – I'd light a candle and burn some incense whilst saying some words of dedication in front of a Buddha image – to set an aspiration to stay on task when distractions arose and as a reminder that I wished to be of benefit in what I did with these devices. Although it's not something I've kept up for long periods at a time, I have found it helpful, especially if I'm becoming aware that I'm getting into bad habits.

One of the advantages of thinking of the cyberloka as a distinct realm is that it enables us to prepare ourselves, to get in the right mental space for it, even to create space for us to ask whether this is the right thing to be doing right now and what we need to be on the lookout for. If I know I'm going out for a nice meal, or a job interview, or a hike in the country, I'll prepare in different ways, because I know that each will require something different of me. One of the main messages of this book is that the cyberloka is another such space, despite how seemingly immediate our transitions into it can be. Entering it involves switching contexts – crossing the threshold into a realm that is designed to be addictive, literalistic, cognitively straining, and superstimulating. And, if we bring enough awareness into that moment, we can prepare ourselves for what we'll encounter – we can even choose whether to do it or not. This, admittedly, is a big ask.

It doesn't come easily to me. But, by periodically reflecting on my screen time, how I use it, what draws me into it, I can make more of this transitionary phase – and apply a better state of mind to it. Bringing greater care to this transition is a straightforward application of Buddhist practice, and it will make the difference between benefiting ourselves and others and descending into distraction.

Questions for reflection and discussion

Think of the last occasion you went on social media – it might be responding to a notification, checking your newsfeed – and see if you can describe the process you went through to end up there. What exactly was the stimulus? What was your emotional and physical state at the time? Where and when was it? What was the result?

How easy or hard is it to reflect in this way? And what might that say about your relationship to social media?

How could you bring greater awareness to your entry into social media or the cyberloka more generally today and this week? Perhaps you could compose a short ritual to mark your first turning towards your devices each day – a couple of sentences and a symbolic action to help you orient yourself more purposefully to what you're doing. You could note down what happened on one or two specific occasions when you went on social media today and share them with someone else reading this book.

To broadcast, or not to broadcast

Right restraint

'And what is right restraint? Here a noble disciple refrains from broadcasting their own negativity and protects themselves from the effects of others' posts.'

As I noted above, social media have given us unprecedented scope for broadcasting ourselves, our opinions, and also – it turns out – our emotions. This gives us a lot of power to influence (and be influenced by) others, for good and ill – trolling[83] being perhaps one of the most egregious forms of the latter (and I'd strongly discourage that, of course). But the practice of right restraint is far subtler and more pervasive than avoiding outright hostility online. It involves becoming aware of our emotional states as we're engaging with our devices, and refraining from sowing seeds of negativity in ourselves and others.

Some psychologists talk about 'online emotional contagion': emotions spread across digital media to others, even in the absence of non-verbals. A now infamous study conducted by Facebook showed that manipulating users' newsfeeds affected their subsequent behaviour:

> When positive expressions were reduced, people produced fewer positive posts and more negative posts; when negative expressions were reduced, the opposite pattern

---

83 '[T]he deliberate act, (by a Troll – noun or adjective), of making random unsolicited and/or controversial comments on various Internet forums with the intent to provoke an emotional knee jerk reaction from unsuspecting readers to engage in a fight or argument.' 'Trolling', available at https://www.urbandictionary.com/define.php?term=Trolling, accessed on 8 February 2022.

occurred. These results indicate that emotions expressed by others on Facebook influence our own emotions, constituting experimental evidence for massive-scale contagion via social networks.[84]

A similar (but more ethical) study found a comparable result on Twitter: positive tweeting was more likely to follow reading others' positive tweets; and negative tweeting, others' negative tweets.[85]

Perhaps this is no surprise – I know how posts involving harsh speech, sarcasm, insensitivity, moaning, and misrepresentation just *make me feel bad* – I seem to absorb the emotional, as well as the literal, content of what is written, whether it be doubt, despair, anxiety, anger, outrage, or whatever. Similarly, posts that are upbeat, celebratory, and joyful can lift my mood.

So taking it as read that it's possible to communicate our emotions across the cyberloka, and the fact that it's possible to reach hundreds or thousands of people instantly, this raises serious questions about what we post. Hopefully it means that we think twice about sharing things out of a negative state of mind – such posts can spread rapidly and widely.

Going back to the parallel with the sexual revolution, this is comparable to the ethics of, dare I say it, *venereal infections*. (To

84 Adam D.I. Kramer *et al.*, 'Experimental evidence of massive-scale emotional contagion through social networks' (2014), available at https://doi.org/10.1073/pnas.1320040111, accessed on 8 February 2022. This study became infamous because it involved tinkering with users' experiences of Facebook without their consent.
85 Emilio Ferrara and Zeyao Yang, 'Measuring emotional contagion in social media' (2015), available at https://doi.org/10.1371/journal.pone.0142390, accessed on 8 February 2022.

coin a phrase, we might even talk about 'textually transmitted dis-ease'.) As with sex, we have a responsibility not to knowingly pass on something that will harm another person, but we also have a responsibility to guard ourselves against exposure to what might harm us. Such is a further application of the ethics of restraint mentioned in Chapter 1.

In this case, it has two aspects: on the one hand, being aware enough of our emotions and holding back from spreading our negativity; on the other hand, picking up the emotional tenor of a post we see and consciously choosing whether or not to engage with it further if it's negative. A few rules of thumb for negativity might be: are we, or they, exaggerating, or speculating about something we/they don't know? Are we, or they, swearing, OR WRITING IN CAPITALS!!? Are we, or they, dwelling on others' faults? Are we, or others, saying things that might lead a third party to form an unfavourable impression of someone? If yes, there's a good chance that it reflects a negative – contracted and unpleasant – state of mind. In Buddhist terms, a negative mental state is defined by greed, hatred, or delusion.

It's hard enough outside the cyberloka to be aware of our mental states and those of others. (Although there is a good chance that, if we're on social media at all, our mental states will be skewed towards the negative.) And it doesn't help that one of the hallmarks of a negative mental state is a certain degree of *un*awareness. Discerning the emotional valence (the positivity or negativity) of words, phrases, and other content in the moment – from us or others – is a skill that takes time and conscious effort to develop. It's a facet of the skill of mindfulness of others. In face-to-face communication, other people often give us cues as to the valence of our communication – at the extremes, they might laugh or wince at what we say. In the cyberloka, however, we largely have to use our imaginations. And some cyberlokans are clearly better at this than others.

On the topic of protecting myself, after a period of reading a lot of online content indiscriminately (and feeling quite emotionally low as a result), I took an unprecedented precept: only to read online content as a 'leisure'[86] activity by those I could imagine trusting enough to have unprotected sex with. My input dropped precipitously. And I felt *amazing*. It's not been all that easy to follow strictly – maybe I just have high standards – but considerations of this kind have certainly led me to prioritize what I do and don't look at.

More broadly as a society, though, having hopefully learned at least some of the lessons of the sexual revolution in relation to our bodily health, we are now starting to ask what lessons we could learn from the digital revolution about our mental health. I'd hazard that the majority of us, probably, would be cautious around the health effects of having unprotected sex with lots of strangers every day. So it can be salutary to recognize, given the studies that now exist on the matter, that the same logic could apply to those we follow in the cyberloka.

This is subtle stuff and probably most of us won't be sensitive enough, enough of the time, to be able to identify the valence of a post anyway (even though we'll doubtless be affected by it). And some cyberlokans will surely cling defiantly to their 'right' to freedom of expression, however

---

86 Sometimes 'work' input doesn't allow for this, though.

fair or foul the results. But for Buddhists I find it interesting that freedom of expression is not a fundamental value: it is subordinate to the values of truthfulness, kindness, helpfulness, and harmony. Speech only has a value insofar as it conduces to *those* values. Otherwise, the Buddha might say, better to keep schtum. What we post does seem to have an emotional effect on others, even if we locate it in the context of an open debate. So we might well ask: how do we create the best emotional conditions for debate? The values I mention don't mean becoming a pushover – if anything, they demand a more vigorous engagement. But in what we view on social media, are we conditioning our minds well for this kind of engagement?

Although more research needs to be done in this area, I believe that routinely and unconsciously absorbing the negativity of others can have far-reaching effects on our mental health, particularly given the volume of content to which we expose ourselves.[87] I've found there to be merit in the practice of restricting my exposure to the online negativity of others, not to speak of sparing others from my own.

But protecting ourselves from others' negativity on social media isn't the end of right restraint. Another aspect of right restraint, we might say, is protecting ourselves from their unrelenting positivity. 'Positivity' perhaps isn't quite the right word, though – more like *perfection*. A few years ago,

---

87 A 2018 study showed that Americans spend approximately eleven hours per day on average looking at screens (I imagine this is now dated and revisable upwards). 'The Nielsen total audience report Q3 2018', available at https://www.nielsen.com/wp-content/uploads/sites/3/2019/04/q3-2018-total-audience-report.pdf, accessed on 8 February 2022.

a friend of mine posted a photo of himself on holiday. It was an aerial shot of him sunbathing. Only it wasn't just him – surrounding him in the image, also sunbathing, were probably about a dozen bronzed young women with flawless 'bikini-ready' physiques. My friend, ordinarily at the moderate end of handsome, looked like he could have been auditioning for a walk-on part in an Australian swimwear commercial. And this was only one of a reel of photos in my newsfeed that day of immaculately groomed, smiling, beautiful, happy people in exotic locations.

I can only speculate as to why *that* image might have stuck in my mind. Aside from wondering how it was that my friend came to be in that photo, I was also struck by the contrast with my own life as I scrolled down my newsfeed that day, the damp November morning pointedly summing up how I was feeling at that time. It can be very tempting when we're faced with a stream of such posts to feel that if our lives – and by this I mean our holidays, dinners, partners, toddlers, tattoos, and dance moves – don't instantly translate into arresting social media posts, then somehow we've failed, we're inadequate. The cyber-dukkha of comparison kicks in. I experience the same thing in watching videos of loquacious, successful people talking about things I feel I should know more about. So guarding our emotional well-being against this kind of thing is perhaps another aspect of right restraint.

Of course, we may simply choose to wish them well and even rejoice in them, if their post reflects a genuinely positive quality they've developed – often the best protection is emotional positivity on our part. Taking this seriously would look like regularly practising the *metta bhavana* and other *brahma viharas*[88] – such practices cultivate the qualities of expansive, warm, encouraging states of mind. These are as much all-round dispositions towards our lives as they are 'emotional' in the narrower sense. And doing them regularly can give us a wellspring of vibrant positive energy from which to meet others.

But we also might remind ourselves, as the waves of perfectionism break over us, that we're *not* seeing the equivalent of their groggy November mornings. Addressing cognitive biases like this is a theme we'll pick up in a later section. In any case, having a clear intention about why we're entering into the realm of social media can give us a helpful anchor when we're liable to be swept away into feeling sorry for ourselves, or may even warn us away from viewing this stuff at all.

All of the above may also give us food for thought about the effect of sharing even what we imagine to be positive posts on social media – subject to the deflationary effect I mentioned above, we can assume that they will land less positively than we had hoped.

In general, though, knowing that emotions can spread to others through our posts means that if we communicate positively – adhering to the facts as best we know them (and signposting when we don't know something), being supportive of others in what we say, and encouraging others to think well of one another – this will have an effect too. Specifically, praising others in ways that indicate that we've really understood them and value what they've done (as opposed to tapping out a lazy 'like') can exemplify a radically

---

88 See Kamalashila, *Buddhist Meditation: Tranquillity, Imagination, & Insight*, Windhorse Publications, Cambridge 2012, pp.139ff.

refreshing way of being on social media, and is much less likely to engender feelings of inadequacy in them. Positive communication like this, rather than simply pleasing our audience or signalling our performance of popular virtues, ultimately means whole communities can flourish. This begins to move in the direction of the ethics of altruism, which we'll look at more in later sections.

Questions for reflection and discussion

How do you gauge whether something you view is positive or negative?

If you've ever 'let off steam' online, what were the effects of doing that for yourself and others?

(How) do you prioritize what you view online? And (how) do you protect yourself from what may harm you?

We should really stop meeting like this...

Right medium

'And what is right medium? Here a noble disciple chooses the appropriate medium in which to post or respond, according to the nature of the message and the strengths and weaknesses of that medium.'

So suppose we're in an emotionally positive state of mind and there is something we want to communicate – how best do we go about it?

Probably we all have our own preferred medium or media in the cyberloka. In itself, that's something worthy of reflection: why is it that I tend to use this medium more than others? It might be because that's where my friends mostly show up; it might be because that's where I feel most comfortable or safe; it might be because I know how to use its features; it might just be because it's fashionable at the moment. Or something else. But I wonder how often we consciously weigh up the pros and cons of particular media before we use them.

One thing that I notice a lot – and again I'd include myself in this – is a strong pull to reply to someone in the same medium in which they posted. Email replies to email; tweet follows tweet; comment, comment. This is undoubtedly the most obvious and convenient thing to do. But it's also, potentially, a missed opportunity.

Not all media are as effective as others for communication. Anthropologists[89] studied people's happiness and laughter while communicating using different media. Although the study is now quite dated (in that some present-day media were not included), they found significant differences between face-to-face, video, phone, email, and SMS[90] texting as different forms of communication. Taking reported happiness and laughter as indicators of social bonding, the data articulate a hierarchy among these media, with face-to-face at the top

---

89 Tatiana A. Vlahovic *et al.*, 'Effects of duration and laughter on subjective happiness within different modes of communication', *Journal of Computer-Mediated Communication* 17:4 (2012), available at https://doi.org/10.1111/j.1083-6101.2012.01584.x, accessed on 8 February 2022.
90 SMS – short message service, a service that allows phones without Internet connection to exchange messages of up to 140 characters.

and SMS at the bottom. Social bonding is essentially about the connection and understanding between people, and clearly some media facilitate this better than others.

I like to think of this in terms of *fidelity*: the faithfulness with which a medium conveys the intentions of the speaker to their audience (and back again). The upshot of this research is that the more a medium is in real time, includes the tone of voice and body language of the people involved (the three Cs of non-verbal communication mentioned earlier), and is free from distractions, the higher its fidelity and the more readily it facilitates connection and understanding.

When we apply this to our social media lives, it appears that there are in fact more or less helpful media for different kinds of communication. Points of information, simple affirmative statements, and long-form think pieces – communications that are less ambiguous and are likely to be received as emotionally neutral or better – are well suited to a text-based medium. But as soon as we enter into ambiguity, nuance, edgy humour, controversy, personal criticism, or anything likely to be received as such, our communication will benefit from recourse to richer, higher-fidelity media such as video calls or face-to-face. Part of what motivated me to write on this topic was seeing how even practising Buddhists could make such a hash of mainly text-based communication – totally misreading each other at times, resulting in an escalation of negativity.

Even face-to-face communication, the highest-fidelity medium of all, requires a great deal of skill and empathy, especially when it enters into more critical territory.[91] As a

---

91 See Shantigarbha, *I'll Meet You There: A Practical Guide to Empathy, Mindfulness and Communication*, Windhorse Publications, Cambridge 2018.

rule of thumb, we could try to respond in the highest-fidelity medium we can, particularly where there is the potential for misunderstanding.

The various lockdowns in the early 2020s amounted to probably the largest-scale uncontrolled experiment of these ideas. When even in-person conversations took place through face masks, we were forced to contemplate, for a period of unknowable length, the possibility of communication without face-to-face. As I mentioned in Chapter 1, I was pleasantly surprised by how effective the various media at our disposal were at allowing us to continue and even initiate substantial talk with one another. Work and other meetings transferred to video calls, and we even began running retreats in this way. Zoom became the default stand-in for what we would previously have done in person.

But it did take some getting used to. Aside from learning the user-level skills (the patience-testing refrain of 'you're muted' being one of the catchphrases of 2020), technical issues made it hard for some people to engage. With dodgy connectivity, audio/visual set-up issues, and the variable lag time between speakers, substituting video calls for face-to-face was often a question of doing the best with what we had. Even after more than a year, the people in my circles still hadn't quite worked out how to deal with those awkward moments in large group calls when everyone's looking at everyone else and no one knows what to say. Others found it all rather tiring (feeling 'Zoomed out' rapidly became a go-to reason to avoid additional social screen time), something I've also heard anecdotally about the advent of the telephone in the early twentieth century. It was perhaps a sign of how things had changed over the intervening century that people would tend to revert to audio-only for relaxing conversations.

My main lesson from this time was that our communication *can* adapt to new circumstances, notwithstanding the initial clumsiness. If it hadn't been for video technology, we would have made audio technology work somehow, I'm sure. But now we are reasonably proficient at a spectrum of different media, we would be wise to ask how best to handle the different options.

The Buddha says that, in addition to considering whether something is true, welcome, and beneficial, he also considers whether it is timely.[92] *Timing* can be crucial to how well our communication lands with the other person (or people). Working in a shared space, or being able to see someone in advance of talking to them, we can often get a sense of whether now is a 'good time' to speak to them. Are they in the middle of something else? Do they seem distracted, stressed? Or are they relaxed, in good humour, and does their body language suggest they'll be receptive to us? Real-time media can give us a chance to sound people out about timing as we go; with other media, we can sometimes leave it to the person to decide when would be a 'good time'. Simply dumping a message in someone's inbox or in a public thread out of the blue (depending on the content of the message) can really jar. On another occasion, a friend of mine sent me an image after he'd been gruesomely injured in an accident – I just opened

---

92 *Abhaya Sutta: To Prince Abhaya (On Right Speech)* (*Majjhima Nikaya*), trans. Thanissaro Bhikkhu, available at https://www.accesstoinsight.org/tipitaka/mn/mn.058.than.html, accessed on 8 February 2022.

my newsfeed and there it was. Although I tried to empathize with what he had been through, I also got the impression that he hadn't thought about how sharing his news in that way might land with his friends.

At our best, we can use the different media at our disposal to respect the content of what we have to say (as well as the people we're talking to). For example, some media will be treated more seriously than others. It's difficult to pin down exactly what I mean by this – it's an aesthetic point. Sometimes the medium will detract from the significance of what we have to share, especially if it's personal or profound. Social media, in general, are quite informal, which lends them to lighter-hearted or less careful communication, which in turn means that this can be how we interpret whatever we see there. If we're trying to communicate something intimate, we might wonder about the effect of juxtaposing it with adverts for protein shakes and dental implants. The same goes for the production value of something we post – it's difficult to appreciate even a very high-quality message delivered with grainy video and poor sound. How and where we post things will influence how well they're received.

Even though I remain impressed and inspired by the potential of social media, my experience of returning to in-person communication after the lockdowns were lifted was one of relief. Once again we had the opportunities for touch, chanting together in unison, and sometimes just enjoying sitting in each other's company. We rediscovered how to laugh along with a large group of people – the secret to comedy, after all, is *not* audio lag. We saw how much easier it is to read people's emotional states when we can see their whole bodies.

And we relished the time to adjourn together afterwards – the non-schedulable idling that completes the arc of any meet-up. This convinced me that online media, as they currently stand, can't be a substitute for face-to-face communication, though, like any technological tool, they can greatly support, supplement, and extend our ordinary capacities. Bearing this in mind, I continue to lean towards the highest-fidelity medium for communication – face-to-face – whenever I can.

Wishing to communicate in ways we hope will be of benefit to others therefore involves being conscious of how our medium of choice affects others' understanding of us and vice versa. I believe that there are better and worse media for facilitating connection and understanding, with face-to-face consistently the best. Perhaps ironically, then, one of the main messages to communicate online is the value of communicating *off*line.

Questions for reflection and discussion

If you have a favourite medium for communication, what is it and why?

In what circumstances do you tend to use video, phone, email, comment threads, instant messaging, SMS, and others? Why? And how do these media help or hinder your communication in the cyberloka?

Are there some things that you would only communicate face-to-face? Why?

For your eyes only

Right audience
'And what is right audience? Here a noble disciple reflects: "Who needs to see this?" and is considerate of their audience, both known and unknown, near and far, born and yet to be born.'

Alongside the question of which medium to use, we might ask who we want to be talking to. In face-to-face interactions, our audience is obvious and we can decide, through the positioning of our bodies, the volume of our voices, and sometimes even the words we choose, who we do and don't want to hear us. As with many of the features of the cyberloka, social media radically expand the spectrum of options available to us, creating a potentially *vast* audience for our thoughts and feelings. This defines the contours of some novel ethical territory, which warrants our reflection.

I, for one, can be drawn in by the sense of affirmation when large numbers of people have interacted with one of my posts. It can be a big hit. But also the hedonic treadmill effect can kick in: over time it takes more and more likes and hearts to provide the same subjective level of affirmation. So it's perhaps understandable that, left unchecked, the gravitational effect in the realm of social media will pull us towards wanting a bigger and bigger audience. This colludes entirely with its 'objective' logic – a bigger audience is just another way of saying more engagement, and more engagement means more advertising revenue. Everything, it would seem, points to us seeking to broadcast to more and more people. Probably this is not such a healthy thing. And

I sometimes wonder how much of the sensationalist one-upmanship I've observed on social media – statements of extreme views, shocking videos, and exhortations to moral purity – can be chalked up to this effect.

Rather than defaulting to this desire for greater exposure, though, we might ask: 'Who actually *needs* to see this?' I find this a challenging question because it compels me to imagine what the needs of my cyber-friends might actually be. For some of them, I'm confident that they might need to know what's going on for me, even without flattering myself – I'm thinking of people like my close friends and family, people who really care about me. But even they could probably get by without seeing a photo of what I had for dinner. What my audience's needs are, and how I might be able to serve them, is often so far down the list of what motivates me to post something that I hardly give it any thought. And, depending on the medium, it can often be difficult to discern their needs even if I wanted to. If I'm honest, what looms largest for me in my cyber-existence is *my* need – to be seen.

That said, there may be times when discussion threads begin to precipitate fresh insights, and we might recognize that 'others may benefit from reading this'. In such cases, though, sometimes the most generous thing would be to summarize the proceedings for others to see, rather than requiring them to trawl through the whole thread themselves and pick out the good bits. Information overload can be wearisome. Even in my own modest friendship circle, if everyone were to post on a daily basis, I'd have the equivalent of a part-time job trying to keep up with it. And that's leaving aside the content from news organizations, celebrities, pundits, and others. Given that we all have the freedom to produce content, we might consider how relevant what we have to say is to the people we're sending it to. I've found it interesting to reflect how the second Buddhist ethical precept (not taking the not-given) might come in here: how might we be taking others' time from them by sending them things they don't need to see?

Even a cursory sweep of the cyberloka's neighbourhoods reveals, for example, ostensibly one-to-one messages taking place in communal forums, or reply-alls whose recipients would rather not be involved. Even assuming that the 'fidelity' of the medium is appropriate for the conversation (see right medium above), there remains the question of whether it needs to be witnessed by that audience. So I try to work on the maxim: *if it's one-to-one, keep it private; if it's public, keep it brief.*

Not that we can totally rely on the privacy of 'private spaces'. Most social media, after all, are just big databases – get hold of the access protocols, and it's yours to search and share what's there. And that's leaving aside the trustworthiness of the people in the spaces themselves. As many of us have found to our cost, a private message is only an indiscreet word or a screen grab away from becoming very public.

So much for the right audience today. But it can also be helpful to remember that once something is online, it's online *forever* (or at least until its deterioration through bit-rot[93] or the eventual demise of the Internet). And, over time, given the propensity for data to 'leak', what might have seemed like fun

---

93 A process whereby digital information becomes corrupted over time.

at the time could be viewed, potentially, by *anyone* – potential employers, our future spouses (or their parents), offspring, pupils, journalists. Knowing this brings an additional layer of mindfulness to my reflections around audience.

Following the parallel with the sexual revolution and being aware of cultural shifts around sex over the last few decades – where in some cases what, at the time, would have been perceived as commonplace behaviour is now viewed as abusive – I'm more than a little curious about how future generations will view our present-day cyberloka activity. As awareness of emotional contagion grows, for example, I wonder how much of what we might consider innocent behaviour today will seem suspect in future years.

What will happen in the digital future is, of course, unknown. And even timely and kindly communication today, taken out of context, may look rather different in years to come. A salutary exercise can be to return to our past posts (most social media have ways of rediscovering our history) and see how they come across in hindsight. Our views can and do change. What we think is worth sharing with everyone can certainly change. And sometimes what we once thought was obvious can point out, in hindsight, a lack of imagination on our part at the time. Notwithstanding the relative permanence of our social data trail, we can make amends by editing or deleting posts, or, where necessary, apologizing for our behaviour to the audiences we've affected.

The big aspiration in this section is to imagine the people who'll receive what we post. Social media increase the different audiences at our disposal, which means we have more complex decisions to make when we choose to share our lives and thoughts. No doubt future generations will roll their eyes at our naivety, but it's our mistakes and learnings that will form the foundations of their (hopefully) greater wisdom in this area.

Questions for reflection and discussion

What does it feel like to you when something you've posted receives likes, hearts, and other reactions? Or even negative reactions? How do these influence the way you then act on social media, in the short and longer term?

How do you decide who to share your communication with? What might you do this week to ensure that the only people who receive communication from you are the ones who need to?

What effect, if any, does the recognition that there are no totally private spaces online have on your online activity?

Say bye-bye to bias

Right cognition

'And what is right cognition? Here a noble disciple is aware of the biases that undermine rational judgement and takes conscious steps to mitigate the effects of these biases.'

While the Buddha of Instagram and the purveyors of toxic conspiracy theories might seem unlikely bedfellows, they do overlap quite naturally in their disdain for clear thinking. Pseudo-Buddhist voices champion the heart over the head – and of course our emotional life is of vital importance too – but often to the extreme of suggesting that the whims of our inner counsel take precedence over everything else. Conspiracy theorists, by contrast, trade off our credulity and make a mess of trying to understand new information themselves. In more dilute forms, too, a lack of clear thinking vitiates the majority of discussions that take place on social media.

Because, although we can quite innocently entertain each other on social media with life events and holiday photos and videos of kittens, these media also play host to a range of conversations on weightier topics – from politics to science to culture. One of the things that drew me to reflect on social media in a more concerted way was the alacrity with which my friends (and 'friends') adopted them as platforms for charged discussions. Being a sensitive soul, I would sometimes feel physically ill from reading the distorted, prejudiced half-truths voiced with absurd confidence – and the emotional reactions from the people they affected.

Let's assume, then, that we wish to tread where saints and angels fear to, and engage in political or cultural discussions on social media. Let's suppose we want to do it skilfully and have chosen, per the previous sections, an appropriate medium and audience. What I hope to do in this section is make a – necessarily brief – Buddhist case for thinking as clearly as we can before attempting to express ourselves.

The Buddha of Instagram is, of course, right that the experience of abandoning the causes of suffering goes beyond words, concepts, logic, and reason. There's even a

Buddhist word for this: *atakkavacara*. But the metaphor of 'beyond' is no accident – it implies that between us and the Buddha's enlightened experience lies clear thinking. Rather than downplaying our reasoning faculty, this metaphor implies that we need to go *through* clear thinking – exhaust it fully – in order to arrive at what lies beyond it. Putting it into more Buddhist language, we need to plumb the depths of 'right view' before we can move on into 'no view'. Even if clear thinking is only a means to an end, it's an indispensable means. And jettisoning it prematurely, or encouraging others to do so, cuts us off from any possibility of development. Perhaps putting it a little strongly, I'd consider this brand of anti-intellectualism to be a kind of violence, since it actively undermines the best for others.

Similarly, the conspiracy theorists are onto something. There *is* more going on than we know – we are often in the dark about things that really matter, and sometimes wilfully so. Again this relates to the Buddhist notion of *avijja*, primordial ignorance, literally 'not-seeing'. Whereas *avijja* is the condition of being out-of-the-know on an existential level, and the Buddhist tradition even suggests that ultimately this is something we choose (though this choice is such a subtle one that most of us aren't aware of it), conspiracy theories often suggest more than this – that someone else is consciously manipulating our access to the truth. Often there is a grain of truth in conspiracy theories – for all sorts of reasons, public figures and organizations withhold information, and media companies feed us only a fraction of what's out there. But along the way conspiracy theorists over-apply this scepticism to their target, so that *anything* they now say is tarnished with the accusation of lies and manipulation, even things that are obviously true and reasonable. As such, conspiracy theories immunize themselves against external critique, treating conciliatory comment as collusion with the malevolent forces they're seeking to expose.

Both the pseudo-Buddhist and the conspiracist flatter us into a state of cognitive laziness: the former by suggesting that thinking is below us somehow, the latter by inducting us into a special club in which we're privy to what ordinary folk aren't. Both are dangerous. They make us vulnerable to being badly misled (and then to mislead others). Being misled, we act in ways that harm ourselves and others. A good grasp of clear thinking, therefore, underpins any benefit we might offer. And it's no easy matter.

This isn't a primer on clear thinking. But knowing how our intuitions and judgements can be misled in a host of predictable ways is a good place to start. Cognitive biases run rampant on social media as we seek to make sense of all the partial or mis-information that is so often the currency in text-based discussion threads. Here, I'll only give a flavour of some of the better-known biases – a drop in the ocean, really – so I'd encourage the reader to consult the burgeoning literature on this subject, beginning with Daniel Kahneman's classic *Thinking, Fast and Slow*.

A humbling rider to all of this, though, is that even if we are aware of these biases, we are almost certainly still going to be subject to them to some degree – and, as always, I include myself in that. Such unawareness has consequences not only for us but also for many others, as the effects of these biases rattle around the cyberloka's echoey spaces.

WYSIATI (What You See Is All There Is)

We human beings are inveterate storytellers, building coherent tales out of as much or as little information as we have. While this often helps us in simple and predictable situations, in environments where our information is patchy or one-sided this can have a number of unfortunate consequences. For example, we can become overconfident in our judgements. Our subjective feeling of confidence in our beliefs increases along with their *coherence* – not their truth. The neater and more emotionally compelling the story we can tell, the more likely we are to believe it. But the irony is that the less information we have access to, the more coherent the story we are able to tell about it (because there is less conflicting information), and therefore the more likely we are to believe it. This is perhaps why the least informed often have the strongest opinions.

Other consequences of this bias are 'failing to account for the possibility that evidence that should be critical to our judgements is missing'[94] and neglecting obvious statistical facts because they are not presented to us. It seems that for most human beings it is just difficult to imagine that we don't have immediate access to all the information.

On social media, where short text-based comments prevail, often the only available information is the literal meaning of what someone has typed. As we saw above, everything else – body language, tone of voice, context, the person's background views, their character, motivations, mood, personal history, and the effects of these on their choice of what is included

---

94 Kahneman, *Thinking, Fast and Slow*, p.87.

or not, sometimes even their identity – may be missing. In this way, we are biased towards creating and propagating believable stories based on what we read in text boxes when in reality this gives us *virtually no* information about the person or the situation as they really are.

A classic example of WYSIATI is *'Nothing's been/being done about it.'* It might be that nothing has been done – but how do we know? Often we jump to this conclusion when in reality we're just not *aware* of what's been done. And this might be for very good reasons – for example, the safety of the people involved. Or sometimes it *was* made public, for good reasons, but a long time ago, perhaps before the advent of the cyberloka (or even our birth). Or sometimes we don't know simply because it's not necessary for us to know – although this can come as an affront to our sense of entitlement. I'd question, going against the received wisdom on many threads, whether transparency is a fundamental value. Sometimes there can be good reasons for not making things public. Whatever the reasons, a lot of concern, and sometimes indignation, accompanies our falling into the trap of WYSIATI.

In 2018 a spoof article cited a study showing that '70% of Facebook users only read the headline of science stories before commenting.'[95] After a short elaboration, which then repeats itself, the article proceeds into 'Lorem ipsum dolor sit amet ...' – *filler*. This apparently didn't stop it being shared and commented upon as if it were the real thing. A genuine study,

---

95 'Study: 70% of Facebook users only read the headline of science stories before commenting' (2018), available at http://thesciencepost. com/study-70-of-facebook-commenters-only-read-the-headline/, accessed on 9 February 2022.

this time on Twitter, found that 59 per cent of the links shared on that platform had never been clicked.[96] WYSIATI and the speed and facility with which information can be shared skew the knowledge ecosystem of social media towards simple and superficial views.

Negativity bias

Sadly, it is often negative stories that show up the most. What we pay attention to, our first impressions, our memories and judgements all predictably overstate the negative. To give an impression of the magnitude of this effect, some psychologists report that, in order to balance out the negativity bias in marriages, couples need to have *five times* more positive interactions than negative ones.[97] Knowing this, we might ask whether we allow for this in what we view online. Hopefully it might also make us more circumspect about arriving at negative conclusions, and in thoroughly weeding out the roots of this bias before sharing them.

This is not to say that we should lump together all criticisms under the heading of 'negativity bias' and avoid having to take responsibility for something that has actually gone wrong and needs dealing with. It's more about recognizing in ourselves that we have a tendency towards negativity, and ensuring that we're not allowing this to exclude other considerations from our view. The critic might want to ask:

---

96 Maksym Gabielkov *et al.*, 'Social clicks: what and who gets read on Twitter?', available at https://hal.inria.fr/hal-01281190, accessed on 9 February 2022.
97 Hara Estroff Marano, 'Our brain's negative bias' (2003), available at https://www.psychologytoday.com/us/articles/200306/our-brains-negative-bias, accessed on 9 February 2022.

what might be the positives as well as the negatives? The person on the receiving end of criticism might ask: ok, so even if it is an expression of negativity, there might be some truth in it, so how can we use this to move forward? Doing this requires imagination and emotional suppleness, but it can save us a lot of angst.

Confirmation bias

Confirmation bias is the 'tendency to search for, interpret, favour, and recall information in a way that confirms one's pre-existing beliefs'.[98] We need less cognitive bandwidth to relate to ideas with which we already agree. This means that if we are feeling lazy or under cognitive strain (both of which can be more likely on social media), we will gravitate towards information, people, and online forums that prop up our view of the world, and ignore or dismiss whatever other views there might be. It's the operation of this bias that can make conspiracy theories so impregnable – their most basic defence, often, is to show how dissent confirms the existence of the evil they're purporting to reveal.

A toxic brew

These biases interact with, and, unfortunately, augment, one another. For example, we'll be more aware of negative information; construct a coherent story around it, which we then believe; and be closed off to new information unless it confirms our story. This makes for a *toxic* brew. On an individual level, we can so easily become entrenched in

---

98 'Confirmation bias', available at https://en.wikipedia.org/wiki/
Confirmation_bias, accessed on 9 February 2022.

unhelpful views that we pick up, getting the wrong end of the stick – at best we look foolish, at worst we make ourselves miserable in the process.

But it has consequences for others too: even the mention of a negative rumour online can quite easily snowball into a damaged reputation, which, for all of the above reasons, can be very difficult to shake off. Sometimes even asking a seemingly innocent question in a public space ('Is it true that X?', if X is something sinister) can start a ball rolling. Once it is rolling, even clarification can be read as defensiveness or a cover-up, and actually further reinforce the negative story in question. And on a bigger scale: outrage-inducing news items, which grab our attention and therefore fit the social media business model, have a habit of swaying public opinion on all kinds of matters. I believe we have a duty not to feed this process.

These biases, like much of what I've been commenting on, long predate the cyberloka. But the cyberloka, and social media in particular, raise the stakes massively. With them we often have less contextual information, less available capacity to stand back and question our views (because, among other things, we're cognitively strained), and greater scope to proliferate our bias-laden thinking to thousands of other people, who in turn are susceptible to all of this themselves. A study conducted on data from Twitter revealed that false news spreads

> significantly farther, faster, deeper, and more broadly than the truth in all categories of information, and the effects were more pronounced for false political news than for false news

about terrorism, natural disasters, science, urban legends, or financial information.[99]

And truthful tweets took, on average, six times as long to spread across Twitter to 1500 users as false ones. The authors of the study suggest that one of the reasons for this might be that false news is often more novel, and our brains are attracted to novelty.

The way to mitigate the effects of these biases for ourselves is to subject our beliefs to rigorous criticism. I regularly revisit the literature on cognitive biases and refresh my understanding of them as a way to bring greater awareness to my thinking. I try to seek out evidence that falsifies my views by checking out a plurality of different news outlets. I work on the *assumption* that I'm under the sway of these biases, and welcome others exposing them in me. I also take steps to limit my exposure to unhelpful views online (see right restraint above) – unfollowing spaces and people I've found to communicate unhelpfully in the past, and only occasionally entering into them, if at all, just to 'gauge the temperature' of the discussion.

It can also be a lot easier to see these biases operating in other people, so if I have views about which I feel uncertain – and especially views about which I feel certain! – I appeal to trusted friends in high-fidelity media (preferably face-to-face) who can highlight whether and how these biases are operating in me. I think that one of the most valuable things we can do

_____

99 Soroush Vosoughi *et al.*, 'The spread of true and false news online', *Science* 359:6380 (2018), pp.1146–51, available at https://www.science.org/doi/10.1126/science.aap9559, accessed on 9 February 2022.

on social media is to build trust and friendship with others in this kind of way.

All of this takes conscious effort and time, as well as humility, to do well. Again, it sets a high bar on the intellectual dimension of our digital responsibility – which most people (like me, if I'm honest) will fall short of again and again – so if we're going to be active in the cyberloka we need to know that doing it well is a tall order.

For this reason, I only very rarely get involved in text-based public online discussions. I just find them far too stressful – hence my writing this book instead. However, sometimes we do need to respond to something in a critical way, which moves us into the arena of right critique.

Questions for reflection and discussion

When you enter a discussion forum or read a news item or post over the next week, you might ask yourself the following questions:

What am I *not* seeing?

Where is the positive story in here?

Am I mistaking the coherence of a story for its correspondence to the facts?

How would I know anyway? Where might I be able to fact-check this? And where did this information originally come from?

What is the effect of bringing these reflections into your life on social media?

A positive feedback loop?

Right critique

'And what is right critique? Here a noble disciple wishes others well and wants to support them in growing beyond their limitations. On this basis, they reflect: "What is the best way to help them?" and give critical feedback only where and when it is necessary and appropriate.'

We can't avoid criticism on social media. It just seems to be part of the fabric of this realm. But that's probably only because it's a feature of human communication more broadly. Even so, criticism does seem to feature unusually prominently on social media. And, following on from the discussion on right cognition, social media often create the conditions for it to escalate into disharmony, ill will, and pain all round. But it doesn't have to be this way. In this section I'm going to look at two of the aspects of critique – the receiving and the giving, what it's like to be criticized on social media, and how to be a critic – and suggest a Buddhist approach to doing these better.

Critique, in the sense of helpful and appreciative feedback, is essential in the flourishing of any community. The advent of the cyberloka has brought with it the technology for entire global communities to be actively involved in this process, with the potential for rapidly developing the life of the community. I believe we've yet to see truly what this can offer, partly because online critique is so often conducted along the lines of finding fault rather than learning from one another. As we'll go on to see, unskilful communication is an obstacle to everyone's learning. A community grows strong, however, when everyone with valuable input feels confident that they will be taken seriously and others are willing to learn from it. But in the meantime we need to learn how to navigate the situations where critique doesn't reach these heights.

On the receiving end

Given the negativity bias, it's likely we'll experience *personal* criticism more acutely online. In the subrealm of social media, where everyone we love and respect can comment and see what others have commented about us, it can be all the more galling to be on the receiving end of a less-than-positive personal remark. We've already seen how titanesque standards of personal appearance can influence us. Being seen to fall short of those standards, even by dint of a lacklustre or ambiguous compliment, or a paltry smattering of likes, can feel punishing. In response, we can be tempted to defend ourselves, hope it blows over, lock away our devices, try to change or hide what's been pointed out, lash out at others, or even lash out at ourselves.

Dealing with comments like this on a practical level can often be fairly straightforward – for the most part they're probably not worth replying to. Assuming they are in fact negatively intended, these kinds of comments often betray the insensitivity or pain of the person issuing them, rather than anything that needs to be followed up by us. Being the victim of sustained and persistent bullying is another matter – and one we'll likely need others' help to overcome.

But I don't think there's an easy solution to the *emotional* fallout from personal criticism online. If we're feeling emotionally robust, it might help to reflect that we're overreacting. But it might not. Even to be able to do this presupposes a strong positive self-esteem independent of online affirmation. If, however, we're entering social media because we're lacking emotional positivity in some way, coming from the hungry ghost or hell realms, then we're opening our sails to the winds of blame and shame. Without supports like the *metta bhavana* and solid, warm relationships beyond our social media activity, we'll be extremely vulnerable to what others say about us. Feeling that vulnerability is probably a reliable indicator that we need to devote more time and energy to those supports, and to cut back our social media activity. Unfortunately we can't control what other people will say about us – this is just another aspect of the logic of the cyberloka (albeit only a more intense version of something we'll always encounter in life) – and if we feel we can't handle what people will say we might want to take a break from it.

Communities in the spotlight

An early motivation for writing this chapter, as I've mentioned already, was seeing some prolonged online disharmony between Buddhists. And, without going into all the details,[100] much of that disharmony centred around my community's culpability for past harms. Suffice it to say that some of the critics had a point. Some of them communicated their concerns with great care. Others, sadly, didn't. But there *was* something that needed addressing – we couldn't just chalk it up to our oversensitivity or others' 'issues'. This is where being on the receiving end of criticism gets much juicier – navigating

---

100 For more information on the theme, I refer readers to https://thebuddhistcentre.com/stories/ethical-issues/about-the-adhisthana-kula/, accessed on 9 February 2022.

the fraught terrain around skilful and unskilful expressions of real grievances, all of which can be heightened on social media. The following is an attempt to summarize some of my learnings from that time.

Although in this section I'm particularly aware of the sangha (the Buddhist community), what I say probably holds for public institutions of all stripes – political organizations, businesses, charities – too. However, social media seem to be especially inhospitable to religious communities at the time of writing. Public confidence in religion is arguably at an all-time low. Intense suspicion colours almost everything religious: religions – perhaps not without good reason – are regarded as cultish, abusive, bigoted, manipulative, power-hungry, patriarchal, corrupt, fraudulent, secretive, and undemocratic; and their members are seen as credulous, idealistic saps. Religious organizations and their leaders are *guilty until proven guiltier*. There's no shortage of vociferous support for anti-religious sentiment on social media.

On top of this, I'd claim that social media structurally privilege superficial fault-finding. Their characteristics of relative anonymity, freedom from being held to account, and speedy, literalistic broadcast communication (from as many people as wish to chip in) favour quick typers with grievances and spare time. The denizens of social media, however, hold the 'official' responses to criticism to a very high standard – and rightly so. But sometimes this holding to account can take the form of a deluge of rapid and prolix comments, each themselves demanding responses. This isn't helped when the comments contain specious arguments, misunderstandings, and misrepresentations that are awkward to leave standing.

Responding thoughtfully takes time and care, but often, by the time the response has finally been composed, the discussion has moved on to something else. Apart from demoralizing the responder, this delay can look bad to the critics, prompting them to claim that they've been ignored. Social media don't make it easy to respond to criticism, and few people are courageous enough to rise to the challenge. To speak of a power imbalance in this environment would be an understatement – many individuals and organizations are *sitting ducks* in the face of cyber-criticism.

Standing up for religious organizations and their members, therefore, is extremely difficult. It's not helped by the contrast between the nature of religion and the nature of social media. This makes the job of embedding a countervailing positive vision for religion in those spaces very challenging indeed. Essentially, the value in religion is *experiential*. It often arises out of the *atmosphere* of people physically coming together on the basis of shared ideals. The language of religion is largely *figurative* – pointing to experiences that are intangible and sublime. Without the kind of preparation we looked at in Chapter 1, it's difficult to communicate the spirit of the religious life in the cyberloka anyway, even to a receptive audience. In a social media environment, though, especially one that's actively hostile, only Buddhas need apply.

That all sounds pretty bad. But, as with the fundamental Buddhist teaching we've been referring to throughout this book, how we experience it is largely to do with the state of mind we bring to it. In particular, a creative mind sees criticism as a buffet of opportunities.

So what are we to do?

The first thing to remember is that we have a variety of media at our disposal (right medium). The higher the fidelity of the medium we choose, the better our responses will land with our critics. From what I've observed, the most effective thing is to relocate the discussion away from social media. We might invite the critics to speak with us in person, or over video – certainly in a higher-fidelity medium than text – and make it clear to everyone else in the forum that this is an option if they wish to follow it up. If they're serious they will take us up on it. We might then return to social media, for example by posting a video of our conversation with a critic. They may have a valid point, which we can learn from (and be seen to learn from), while demonstrating that we're human beings too and really not that evil after all. Videos give a lot more contextual information than a written statement – the sincerity of an apology, for example, is likelier to come across when congruent with our behaviour, tone of voice, and expressions than in a text box.

Criticism is an opportunity, albeit one that we're likely to experience as unpleasant. Critics demand a response, which is a way of initiating communication with us, and communication is always a positive opportunity – to connect, learn, exemplify. If, for example, skilful communication is something we value, criticism gives us a public platform to showcase this, as well as any other values we hold dear. I know people who, having encountered the way my friends and I responded to the criticisms of our community, became *more* inspired to join us. I find it fascinating, and maybe even a bit paradoxical, that we can actually exemplify our best when we're sorting out our worst.

There's no formula for this beyond patience and a willingness to enter into two-way communication. We're not actually at the mercy of our critics if we see their interventions as an excuse to display what's best in us. We don't have to satisfy every critic either. My own teacher, Urgyen Sangharakshita, who was no stranger to criticism for most of his ninety-three years, spoke of the value in *tolerating dissent*. Even if we agree that our critics are onto something, we may justifiably disagree over what to do about it. So we're never going to eliminate criticism altogether, even from our friends. But some people will question what we do or say, simply because we do or say it, or because they enjoy questioning, or because they have totally unrelated, but unresolved, issues that manifest as criticism. What this asks of us, if we're on the receiving end of such criticism, is to be able to step back enough from its 'sting' to be able to discern whether we have in fact acted badly and how to make amends if so. It asks us to look at whether the mental states we've brought to our actions have culminated in suffering, for ourselves or others. Here, two-way discussion can be vital, especially when charting the waters of novel ethical grey areas (which the cyberloka has a habit of unearthing). The alternative is to capitulate to every criticism, entailing an endless, probably contradictory, list of demands that'll likely take us further and further away from our goals. Seeing criticism as a way to move towards those goals, however, reframes the situation entirely.

How to critique
So much for responding to critics. We may also find ourselves, perhaps tentatively, wishing to enter into a critique of others.

To do this well requires skill. In the first place, right critique, in the sense of thoughtful, helpful, appreciative, and sensitive criticism, *takes time*. (This chapter is part of a years-long process of trying to understand and critique the difficulties I've seen on social media.) Right critique involves teasing out and challenging assumptions, celebrating merits as well as highlighting shortcomings, being able to clarify what is unclear, and doing all of this with a sensitivity to our own needs, the needs of the other people involved, and those of a potentially large unknown audience.

Right critique is also reflexive: involving an awareness of ourselves, our motivations for critiquing, and the extent to which we're also guilty of what we see in others. And even when we take all of this into account, it can still be badly received. The so-called 'backfire effect',[101] where attempts to critique actually reinforce others' unhelpful views, is just one example of how things can go wrong. And, as we saw under the heading of right cognition, some views are almost booby-trapped against external influence.

As with so much of skilful communication on social media, we're seriously up against it: in moments of laziness or lapses of mindfulness it's so easy just to lob a cheap put-down into a public space or angrily reply-all and simply fan the flames of cyber-dukkha. And our attempts at right critique can be all too easily frustrated by all the aspects of the logic of the cyberloka we've touched on so far. Right critique is not easy at all.

But it's important to do well: when we critique unskilfully, it silences genuine discussion. False, harsh, unhelpful, and

---

101 'Backfire effect', available at https://en.wikipedia.org/wiki/ Confirmation_bias#backfire_effect, accessed on 9 February 2022.

slanderous speech – even if we can cleverly rationalize them – will undermine people's trust in one another and result in defensiveness, point scoring, polarization, and eventually good people not wishing to be involved. Warning bells should ring if considerate, warm-hearted people start checking out of an online space – it suggests that the conditions do not support genuine discussion. Ultimately, that means that critical voices will be ignored too, which in the long run may actually make a difficult situation worse.

Creating the space

So even before we enter into right critique, we need spaces in which genuine discussion can take place, where people aren't afraid of losing face in front of others and there is an atmosphere of mutual support, curiosity, and learning. These might be spaces that we create ourselves, or ones that we transform over time – though it's much harder to shift an existing culture. The kind of qualities in such a space will include (but not be exhausted by) the following.

APPRECIATION

This refers to naming, and drawing attention to, specific things in others that merit praise. Not doing this simply in order to flatter them into agreeing with us – which they'll see through anyway – but because an atmosphere in which rejoicing takes place is an essential condition for learning. The state of mind called *mudita* (altruistic joy), in which we intensify our awareness of others' ethical strengths, is a potent social glue and a perfect basis on which to then broach trickier matters.

BUILDING RAPPORT

This involves taking an interest in how others are doing and what's going on in their lives to remind ourselves that they are human beings after all, rather than just thumbnails disgorging text. I've also seen people talk a bit about their own lives ('Just got back from the shops on a beautiful sunny morning') before entering into the discussion. It's salutary that almost always before giving a discourse the Buddha would engage in 'courteous and amiable' talk with those he was entering into dialogue with – basic pleasantries, the details of which were rarely recorded, unfortunately. Nonetheless, this was all about building rapport.

CHALLENGE

We need to encourage people in the space to want to grow, and to see their views being challenged as a way to do this. Also it's a matter of being prepared to be challenged ourselves, even seeking out challenges to our existing views. Going in with a genuine question to the effect of 'I think I'm missing something here, can someone fill me in on ... ?' is one of scores of ways of eliciting helpful feedback. In effect, this exemplifies a mature relationship to *avijja* (ignorance) that makes it possible for everyone else to admit to gaps in their understanding.

DANA (GENEROSITY)

This may be explicit offers of help, or simply a willingness to be of service to others should the opportunity arise. It's also an attitude of not merely being a spectator – much less a sniper – but, if circumstances require it, being an active participant in whatever concrete action needs to follow a critique. Assuming we want to be of benefit, it's not enough simply to criticize from a safe distance and leave it to others to pick up the pieces.

EXEMPLIFICATION

This means that our digital behaviour is impeccable and that others can look to us in many different ways for guidance on how to relate to one another. Our kindness, contentedness, awareness, imagination, creativity, availability, and so on should come out in everything that we do – not just what we say. For example, when giving critical feedback online we might exemplify the following good practice, drawing on previous sections:

- Choosing the medium well:
  - Preferably in real time.
  - Allowing body language and tone of voice to be communicated (right medium).
- If we're named in an online discussion and need time to reflect and compose a response, indicating this in the discussion thread, along with a provisional time by which people can expect to hear back.
- If using long-form text, sending a draft of the critique in a one-to-one space (right audience) and some way in advance, to give our interlocutors time to peruse and respond before we post anything publicly.
- Remembering that criticism is rarely pleasant to receive, and that unsolicited public criticism is frequently *horrible* and likely to be reacted against (right restraint).

* * *

In addition to the 'emotional' qualities of spaces in which right critique can flourish, if we're using text, some 'forms' support it better than others. For the most part, text-based discussions follow the form of an opening post and a free-for-all comments thread, more or less moderated. As someone who routinely leads in-person discussion groups, I know that hoping that a helpful conversation will emerge from a context like this is wishful thinking. It's at the mercy of the good will and skill of the individuals involved, some of whom may be trolls or other kinds of bad actors. Below I give just a handful of examples of other forms we might draw on, for different purposes, to support our text-based discussions.

OPINION GATHERING

In some organizations,[102] decision makers post ideas on their internal blog as a way to sound out their co-workers. The format actively invites critique as a way of finding out the opinion of the organization before making a big decision – it may be that a clear view emerges, or that further thought is needed, but this can be a very helpful device for leaders to 'gauge the temperature' of the organization on a particular theme. This also *deploys* the latent critical faculty of the organization in its own service, which if left idle can sometimes mutate into an organizational autoimmune disease. Responses may be expected to be stated without cross-dialogue, or it may be that some interaction is allowed within certain limits.

---

102 See the presentation of Buurtzorg, a Dutch neighbourhood nursing company, in Frederic Laloux, *Reinventing Organizations: A Guide to Creating Organizations Inspired by the Next Stage of Human Consciousness*, Nelson Parker, Brussels 2014.

PRODUCT FOCUS

Wikipedia[103] is the paragon of this kind of discussion – here the purpose of the conversation is to arrive at a public-facing product of some kind. The discussion achieves focus through the aim of producing publication-standard material. Alternatively, the standard merely needs to be known and shared between the collaborators and the recipients of the product so there can be an objective arbitrator when disputes arise.

Q&AS

Here an individual may subject themselves to questioning from a cyber-audience – the restrictions may involve posting the questions in advance and vetting them, a maximum length of question, and a time frame for participation. The individual provides the focus and direction that the discussion can then lead in.

VARIABLES TO PLAY WITH

Each of these forms highlights that there are a number of variables that we can tweak depending on the kind of discussion we want to have and the ends to which we want to put it. These are things like: the way we frame the topics, the ethos that we hope to share, the time frames involved, who joins the discussion, and the quantity and quality of responses.

So, for example, we might kick off the conversation in a variety of ways: referring to an article, telling a story, or simply asking a question. Learning the art of a good question is key

---

103 A free online encyclopedia: www.wikipedia.org.

to facilitating discussions of all kinds: open questions invite people to explore and elaborate on their views; questions that force the audience to hold seeming contradictions create curiosity. Any question, though, will shape the conversation, and we can use this fact to steer it in the direction of depth, rather than proliferation.

Then there are things we might want to encourage in the participants' responses: things like the appreciation, building rapport, challenge, dana, and exemplification we mentioned above. But we might also want to invite people explicitly to draw out each other's points, to build on what others have said, and to bring in elements of their offline lives that might contextualize their thoughts.

We might want to strengthen deeper thinking on a particular topic. So, rather than inviting immediate reactions, we might request that people respond only after twenty-four (or forty-eight or seventy-two) hours. Similarly, we could limit the number of posts people can make within a time frame – a maximum of once every twenty-four hours (or even once per month) might mean that people are more considered in how they contribute to the discussion. The discussion might also have a start and an end time so as to add extra focus and make it into more of an event.

We might want to decide who can participate in the discussion – perhaps people with certain qualifications or experiences – while making the discussion visible (or not) to others. We might stipulate that posts have to reach a certain standard of writing. The AskPhilosophy subreddit,[104]

104 'AskPhilosophy', available at https://www.reddit.com/r/askphilosophy/, accessed on 9 February 2022.

for example, allows anyone to ask a question but expects scholarly responses – including the use of references and citations. Clearly this will require more work on the part of the moderators, but the results speak for themselves.

We might want to restrict the length of responses – say, fewer than 100 words if we only want simple responses, or more than 500 words if we want to encourage more substantial contributions. We might want to avoid rambling responses by requesting that contributors make only one point per post.

There are lots of ways in which we can shape the conversation space along these lines – to encourage quicker or slower responses, more or fewer participants, longer or shorter contributions. Each of these will offer different benefits, depending on what it is we're hoping to achieve from the discussion, whether it's a quick survey of people's views or a thoughtful collective examination of a topic.

My observation of viewing a lot of online discussions is that often there's little to no thought given to what might be achieved from them, beyond the vague value of sharing views. I think this is a wasted opportunity. Where there is more of a conscious direction to a discussion, just as with in-person sessions, we're better at building on what others say, holding others to account, and developing our thinking, critical or otherwise. Having clear guidelines to the discussion, in particular, gives people the confidence to stand up to behaviour that is not in the interests of the conversation. There are potentially so many different permutations for the kinds of discussions that can draw on the immense information-gathering potential of the Internet – I'd love to see more people creating the spaces in which structured conversations can take place online.

In short, what I'm describing is a shift in the metaphor from *posting* to *hosting* – from, as it were, nailing our critical remarks to a post for all to see to hosting the kinds of conversations in which criticisms can be voiced, heard, and addressed. In my experience, this requires being more direct and explicit about the parameters than when hosting in-person discussions, where much can be conveyed implicitly.

From conflict to contact

Finally, on this theme, critique often goes hand in hand with disagreement and conflict. The evolutionary origins of humanity's mechanisms for resolving conflict offer some pointers here. In non-human primates – those animals that most closely resemble humanity's evolutionary ancestors – conflict resolution typically involves some kind of physical contact.[105] For example, chimpanzees kiss and embrace after fights. Other great apes groom one another or allow an intermediary to groom each party before the two reconcile. In human society, there is the customary handshake at the end of a sports match, or make-up sex after a romantic tiff. Knowing this, I'd champion the role of physical contact in bringing online disagreements to a conclusion. But this is one thing the cyberloka cannot offer. So we would be wise to conduct critique in person as much as possible – for all the many supports that that can give but also because, in the event of conflict, physical contact, if genuinely coming from a place

---

105 Frans B.M. de Waal, 'Primates: a natural heritage of conflict resolution', *Science* 289:5479 (2000), pp.586–90, available at http://science.sciencemag.org/content/289/5479/586, accessed on 9 February 2022.

of reconciliation, can help all parties to move on together in harmony.

Questions for reflection and discussion

In your experience, which existing online spaces have best supported right critique? What have they done practically to bring this about?

Have you ever been on the receiving end of cyber-criticism, in public or in private? How did you handle it, and what did you learn from the experience?

Have you ever attempted to give critical feedback to other people on social media? How did it go, and what might you do to improve it in future?

From cyber-dukkha to cyber-bodhi?

Right recollection

'And what is right recollection? Here a noble disciple does not engage in the various kinds of pointless comments, that is, comments about kings, thieves, and ministers of state; comments about armies, dangers, and wars; comments about food, drink, garments, and beds; comments about garlands and scents; comments about relations, vehicles, villages, towns, cities, and countries; comments about women and men, and comments about heroes; street comments and comments by the well; comments about those departed in days gone by; rambling chitchat; comments about the world and about the

sea; comments about becoming this or that. Rather, a noble disciple recollects the Dhamma and comments about cyber-dukkha, its origin, its cessation, and the path leading to its cessation.'

This is a transposition of what the Buddha describes as 'idle speech' into the idiom of the cyberloka ('comments' replacing 'speech'). The Buddha of the Pali Canon clearly doesn't have any truck with this, and I shudder to think what he would make of a lot of what we say and share on social media.

I'm not saying that none of this has worth, though. It's more that discussions on these topics tend to remain on the same level, rather than going deeper into material that might actually change something for somebody, along the lines of Chapter 1. I've observed this sort of thing online for more than a decade; it so often goes nowhere. The protagonists, rather than seizing the opportunity of communication to disrupt their fixed views and habitual patterns, mostly just trot them out – that is, until everyone gets bored and moves on to another thread. The broadcasting of entrenched mental states, applied now to this topic, now to that, is a classic example of the horizontality I mentioned in Chapter 1.

Of course, we are free to engage in these discussions if we wish, just as we are free to do anything (Buddhism is not a commandment-based religion). However, we would be wise not to lose track of the real purpose that the Buddha has for communication.

And let's cut to the chase here: this purpose isn't to put the world to rights. It's doubtful it'll happen anyway, no matter how many little text boxes we fill in our attempts. What the Buddha encourages us to recollect again and again is how to overcome suffering and its causes. We do this by seeing how we cause ourselves dukkha in our cyclical mental states and behaviours, and stepping out of them (à la Arahant Ideal). And helping others to do that for themselves, where we can (à la Bodhisattva Ideal).

I notice, even in 'Buddhist' spaces, how we can devote so much energy to addressing the worthy issues of the day, but virtually everyone seems to take the cyberloka itself for granted. Which is a great shame because, as we've seen, far from being a neutral space designed to facilitate thoughtful discussion, it has its own distinctive effects on our minds and the unhelpful cycles we can get stuck in. In attempting to right the wrongs of the world at large, we can so easily lose sight of what's under our very noses: the unsatisfactoriness of *the cyberloka*, its causes, the possibility of freedom, and the path leading to freedom. In doing so, we forget the Buddha's purpose, however worthy our discussions might be according to other standards.

In this connection I'm reminded of the depictions of the bodhisattvas in the realms of the Wheel of Life, and how they hold or model the antidote to the cyclical patterns in each of those realms.

I wonder, then, what the bodhisattva might hold in the cyberloka 2.0?

Before addressing that question, three paths to freedom suggest themselves. In brief: purifying social media; liberation into the human realm; and *cyber-bodhi*, awakening directly from the cyberloka.

Purifying social media

Although at times I've been quite critical of the cyberloka, I actually have high aspirations for it as a medium for us to connect and communicate with one another. This is why this is a book, rather than a short one-sided takedown. I have seen examples of meaningful discussions in which multiple parties arrive at an understanding of each other and grow through the interaction. I have enjoyed the opportunities for connection afforded by more convenient media. And I continue to see creative ways of using the spaces on social media to further ideals that exceed their boundaries.

More often than not, the positives I've encountered stem from skilful communication. At the highest level of generality, the four Buddhist speech precepts sketch out the features of this kind of communication:

- I undertake the training principle to refrain from false speech /
  With truthful communication I purify my speech.
- I undertake the training principle to refrain from harsh speech /
  With kindly communication I purify my speech.
- I undertake the training principle to refrain from idle speech /
  With helpful communication I purify my speech.
- I undertake the training principle to refrain from slanderous speech /
  With harmonious communication I purify my speech.

But the *spirit* of these precepts is what really matters – it's not simply a question of sticking legalistically to their letter. In fact, it's possible to pay lip service to all of the above in a post but actually be coming from quite a negative place. And it shows. The spirit of the speech precepts is to create an atmosphere in which people take one another seriously, in which it is possible to empathize and enter into one another's point of view, and in which mutual learning can therefore take place. Ultimately, the speech precepts build trust and curiosity and warmth and depth between us. It's about more than just minding our digital Ps and Qs. And it's about more than being ostentatiously 'deep'.

I see criticism and challenging each other as intrinsic to this atmosphere too: genuine discussion and learning will inevitably involve elements of challenge and, if it's done in the spirit of these precepts, everyone benefits.

Other ways to purify social media might be to introduce explicitly Buddhist content – videos, audio, images, animations, podcasts, live-streaming events – getting helpful and clear Buddhist teachings into circulation. (There's a lot of quite misleading material out there, most notably the 'fake Buddha quotes' I mentioned earlier – attributions of pseudo-psychology and anachronistic political views to the Buddha – which undermine his radically different take on life.) At the moment, there's a huge potential audience for intelligent and well-produced Buddhist content, and there's massive scope for creativity in this field.

Finally, on purifying social media, it's not so much about developing a Buddhist commentariat on contemporary issues (this book aside) – for a start, I'm not sure there is 'a' Buddhist comment on any contemporary issue – than about exemplifying a better kind of communication, one that is aware of the potential pitfalls and is able to navigate them skilfully to everyone's advantage. In this vein, I'd like to see more of us reflecting on the way in which the prevailing online environment affects our ability to connect and communicate – for example, 'this medium isn't working for me, would you be up for a video chat?' or 'I'm finding it difficult to empathize with you, can you tell me a bit more about what's going on for you right now?' Social media, in and of themselves, do have an astonishing potential for connecting people – and I'd like to see more Buddhists leading the way on how to do this.

Liberation into the human realm

That said, a lot of the psychological research I've mentioned points to the advantages of face-to-face contact as a way of overcoming some of the difficulties with online communication. The human realm, as symbolizing a state of balance and level-headedness, can be the most direct way to arrive at those liberating experiences of depth and pleasure that we saw in Chapters 1 and 2, and as such should be our baseline, if we have a choice. One of the main stabilizing factors in the human realm is the human body itself – grounding our communication in embodied awareness is therefore a ready route to the human realm.

We can, of course, use our social media activity to exemplify and encourage this kind of embodied communication. This might come in the form of publicity for in-person activities or videos of friends talking over current affairs together.

Indirectly, it might look like tips for how to manage our screen time in proportion to face-to-face interactions.

As something of an aside here, Buddhism has got some major work to do on its online image. Put 'Buddhism' or 'meditation' into image searches, and typically you'll get photos of oriental monks, svelte yogis in full-lotus position silhouetted against a sunset, and flowers with dewy petals. And these images tend to be the ones that appear in Buddhist event publicity. What these images fail to show is that Buddhist practice is a path of rigorous activity, effort, determination, and, on the basis of that, *surrender*. It's a challenge that, while undoubtedly beautiful at times, can also be quite gritty at others and points to an ideal that, as I've gestured at, far exceeds our ordinary habits. It's also, crucially, something collective, done in the company of others. Speaking a little loosely, Buddhism probably has more in common with elite sport than with a spa weekend, and yet Buddhism's visual vocabulary still leans on the latter. A big part of liberating folks into the human realm will involve presenting an arresting and attractive case on our screens for why there's more to be had *off* them.

Cyber-bodhi

But, beyond this, no loka from the Buddhist perspective is 'holy', not even the realm of the long-lived gods. All realms have their defining cyclical patterns – their dukkha – which hint at how to go beyond dukkha altogether. Buddhism's aim, either through the ethics of restraint or through altruism, isn't simply to rotate from one realm to another, but to see the unsatisfactoriness of being en-realmed. Re-becoming, whatever its forms, is an existential situation defined by dukkha in more or less obvious ways, and the Buddha's message is that liberation from this existential dukkha is possible. In some ways, though, social media may be a trickier launchpad for this: we can be so distracted and overstimulated that we find it harder to see the subtle – or even not-so-subtle – clues that something is amiss, and that the deepest depth, bodhi, the awakening of the Buddha's experience, is possible. This goes as much for ourselves as for our attempts to help others.

But I wonder, at the risk of being fanciful, whether the logic of social media offers us an obvious basis to reflect on our existential situation in general. This could even tally with the three *laksana*s, or marks of conditioned existence, which the Buddha invites us to explore in all realms, presumably even including the cyberloka.

First, as we've seen, the phenomena of the cyberloka are transitory, ephemeral, *impermanent*. We can reflect on how quickly things seem to move on online – and that this is not just true online. Deeper reflection reveals that this characteristic is true of all phenomena whatsoever. We cannot grasp or retain anything indefinitely, and it is futile to try to do so. Recognizing the flow of phenomena isn't just an antidote to FOMO but can liberate us from our sticky attachment to things (by which I mean: stuff, people, ideas, status, and so on) more generally.

Second, much goes on in the cyberloka over which we have little control – whether it's receiving criticism, the stimulation of desires for things and people we'll never have, or the explosion of content beyond our capacity to respond to it. We can't fix these features of the cyberloka – it's *inherently unsatisfactory*. Reflecting on this we can see that in fact the whole of our experience cannot be made to conform with our ideas and preferences. Trying to fix it often only makes its unsatisfactoriness stand out more. When we see this more deeply, we learn to let go of this desire to control and fix, and to abide in our direct experience as it presents itself.

Third, and finally, we can reflect that no phenomenon in the cyberloka is our own – once I've posted something, it's out there for anyone else to share and use for their own purposes. And anything I post has almost certainly come from somewhere else – I can't really take the credit for any of my ideas if I'm totally honest. Taking this to the next level, I see that this is true not only with my *bons mots* on a thread, but with the totality of what I think of as 'me': 'my' physical form, 'my' thoughts, 'my' possessions. All this has come from what is not me and, at some point, will pass again into what is not me, although I will identify with it to a greater or lesser extent in the meantime. Reflecting on the nature of the cyberloka in this way, I can see that, independently of the nexus of conditions flowing around, there is *nothing I can point to as a 'me' or as 'mine'* in any ultimate sense. Such a realization begins to open up the possibility of liberation from the cyberloka, and eventually from self-made suffering of all kinds.

And what does that liberation from the cyberloka look like? *'What is the cessation of cyber-dukkha? The remainderless logging off, renunciation of accounts, relinquishment of devices, release and letting go of that very craving.'* The 'remainderless logging off' is the state of leaving the cyberloka and feeling like there is nothing more that ties us to it, nothing compels us to return to it. The 'renunciation of accounts' decouples us from our online personae, we no longer feel the urge to keep up appearances. The 'relinquishment of devices' might be what it's like to realize, happily, that we can't even remember where we put our device – we're free to pick it up and put it down at will, *we're using it*, not the other way around. And then there's the 'release and letting go of that very craving' – a release from our attachment to the stimulation, affirmation, and novelty of social media, and a contentedness that radiates from within us.

All of this points to a freer way of being within the cyberloka – a freedom, that is, to engage with it or not, depending on what is of benefit. To be absolutely clear, liberation from the cyberloka doesn't mean condemning it, or even necessarily avoiding it. Nor am I suggesting that the Buddhist take on social media is just to log off permanently or return to a prehistoric kind of existence. It's more about not taking the cyberloka so seriously – not being so much at the mercy of its attractions and imperatives. Not being caught in its predictable cycles. We know we're liberated when we're able to put our devices to sleep without feeling the need to wake them up again. We know we're liberated when we can enter social media without feeling the need to stay there out of a fear of missing out. It's about the freedom to decide what we make of our lives, to be in control of our devices rather than the other way around, and to be able to discover deeper sources of satisfaction.

Maybe the Buddha would have entered the cyberloka – the *Facebook Sutta* certainly invites us to imagine that he did – but he would have been realistic about the effects of doing so on him, and not have got trapped in the cycles of grasping or aversion within it. On that basis, he might have been able to offer some help to the people he would have met there. The Buddhist approach to digital life, I think, breaks down into three things: understanding the logic of the cyberloka, freeing our minds from the unhelpful habits it can encourage, and only then beginning to open up possibilities of freedom to others.

What the bodhisattva holds

As we saw in Chapter 2, in each of the six realms of the Wheel of Life, a bodhisattva of a different colour appears, offering to the beings in that realm something they need. So the questions arise: what colour is the bodhisattva in the realm of social media, and what does he hold?

Taking the questions in reverse order, we might say that the bodhisattva actually holds three things, although two of them slightly stretch the metaphor of 'holding'. First, the bodhisattva purifies the cyberloka. He does this by *holding the space* – by creating and maintaining conditions in which we can communicate meaningfully with one another. Second, the bodhisattva liberates beings into the human realm. He does this by *holding out his hand* to them – offering them face-to-face communication, physical contact, and friendship. Third, the bodhisattva points out the way to *cyber-bodhi*. He does this by *holding up a mirror* – enabling us to reflect on the logic of the realm we're in and how this points to something beyond it.

And the bodhisattva's colour is amber, a deep, warm yellow-orange-brown, the colour of fossilized tree resin. Sangharakshita associates the colour amber with the precept of kindly speech and the creation of 'an atmosphere of positivity within which spiritual friendship can develop and the spiritual life can be led'.[106] Amber as a substance is also remarkable because it can hold an electric charge – a quality that, in the often-divisive world of cyberloka discussions, is a strength indeed.

> ## Questions for reflection and discussion
>
> What have you commented on recently on social media? And why did you do it?
>
> What might you do over the coming week to communicate a positive vision of life (Buddhist or otherwise) on social media?
>
> Take a few moments during the day to reflect on the 'nature of existence' in the cyberloka: the pace at which things change, the inability of our online experiences to satisfy us, and the way in which we can never ultimately own the content we meet. What effect do these reflections have on the way you approach your digital life?

---

106 Sangharakshita, *The Three Jewels I* (*The Complete Works of Sangharakshita*, vol.2), Windhorse Publications, Cambridge 2019, p.380.

Postscript

I haven't attempted to give an exhaustive treatise on the cyberloka. Inevitably, as I've already mentioned, there are limitations to what I can say about it. In particular, I'm conscious that I've not addressed the 'systemic' dimension of our digital lives. This is mainly because I don't know much about it. So I've decided to leave what I do know and think about it to this postscript. I'm aware that prominent figures in the digital world are coming forward to demand greater regulation of social media. They want to level the battlefield in the war between the supercomputers and the humble human brain. All of which I thoroughly support. As individuals, we can be naive and slow to adapt to changes in our social world; legislation can lag even further behind. And it's interesting to note, at the time of writing, the efforts of the Chinese government to limit the power of big-tech-with-Chinese-characteristics and lessen its negative effects on their youth. This is still at a very early stage, and no doubt more questions will arise as that project evolves.

But I also want to sketch out why we cannot rely solely on regulation to rectify the situation for us. In short, if social media weren't ensnaring our attention, endangering our children, or undermining the very fabric of society, well, something else would be. Social media are only the most visible and successful exploiters of our all-too-human susceptibility to intoxication, disharmony, and credulity – or greed, hatred, and delusion, to give them a more Buddhist gloss. So long as we leave these 'unwholesome roots' untouched, we'll continue to be vulnerable to malevolent forces intent upon subjugating us for their own profit; we'll also still find ourselves in painful situations of our own making. I agree that social media seem to raise the sophistication of our dukkha to an altogether new – and even alarming – level, but we're always up against *something* in this regard. Again, the teaching of the six realms of the Wheel of Life reminds us that no realm is without its intrinsic dukkha, whether it's explicitly programmed in or not.

I've learned enough over the years to know that I've still got a long way to go in overcoming these forms of dukkha. At the very least, my reflections have disabused me of some of my initial naivety: about the cyberloka's effects on me and my ability to affect others in this realm. I hope what I've written will give you food for thought. Personally, I've taken conscious steps to guard the 'gates of my senses' both on- and offline. The issues with the cyberloka are not peculiar to it – they speak to our basic dispositions, which take concerted personal effort to overcome. And I'm convinced that any attempts to address dukkha on a more systemic level need to take this personal dimension into account.

I say this because, regulation or not, technological remedies or not, the starting point for these reflections remains the same. It hinges on the kind of mind we bring to our digital lives. Expansive, warm, lucid, generous minds make mature use of the tools of the cyberloka. Tight, anxious, dull, stingy minds *become the tools* of their algorithmic overlords. Regulation might dampen the cynical impulses coming our way, but nothing short of learning how to deal with impulses *per se* is going to offer us security beyond that. This has profound implications for what I've been calling the two ethics of restraint and altruism – both come down to the question: what's going on in our minds? Gaining increasing clarity on this, we might start to venture with confidence into rancorous or highly stimulating spaces, and even make a positive difference there. Lacking clarity on this, we hand our lives over to whoever plies us with clickbait.

WINDHORSE PUBLICATIONS

Windhorse Publications is a Buddhist charitable company based in
the United Kingdom. We place great emphasis on producing books
of high quality that are accessible and relevant to those interested in
Buddhism at whatever level. We are the main publisher of the works
of Sangharakshita, the founder of the Triratna Buddhist Order and
Community. Our books draw on the whole range of the Buddhist
tradition, including translations of traditional texts, commentaries,
books that make links with contemporary culture and ways of life,
biographies of Buddhists, and works on meditation.

As a not-for-profit enterprise, we ensure that all surplus income
is invested in new books and improved production methods, to
better communicate Buddhism in the 21st century. We welcome
donations to help us continue our work – to find out more, go to
windhorsepublications.com.

The Windhorse is a mythical animal that flies over the earth carrying
on its back three precious jewels, bringing these invaluable gifts to
all humanity: the Buddha (the 'awakened one'), his teaching, and the
community of all his followers.

Windhorse Publications
38 Newmarket Road
Cambridge CB5 8DT
info@windhorsepublications.com

Consortium Book Sales & Distribution
210 American Drive
Jackson TN 38301
USA

Windhorse Books
PO Box 574
Newtown NSW 2042
Australia

THE TRIRATNA BUDDHIST COMMUNITY

Windhorse Publications is a part of the Triratna Buddhist Community, an international movement with centres in Europe, India, North and South America, and Australasia. At these centres, members of the Triratna Buddhist Order offer classes in meditation and Buddhism. Activities of the Triratna Community also include retreat centres, residential spiritual communities, ethical Right Livelihood businesses, and the Karuna Trust, a UK fundraising charity that supports social welfare projects in the slums and villages of India.

Through these and other activities, Triratna is developing a unique approach to Buddhism, not simply as a philosophy and a set of techniques, but as a creatively directed way of life for all people living in the conditions of the modern world.

If you would like more information about Triratna please visit thebuddhistcentre.com or write to:

London Buddhist Centre
51 Roman Road
London E2 0HU
United Kingdom

Aryaloka
14 Heartwood Circle
Newmarket NH 03857
USA

Sydney Buddhist Centre
24 Enmore Road
Sydney NSW 2042
Australia

Entertaining Cancer
The Buddhist Way
Devamitra

You're diagnosed with an aggressive cancer – what do you do?

Devamitra – English actor and Buddhist teacher – describes the discomforts and indignities of being treated for prostate cancer. He draws on the deep well of his Buddhist practice to work with his mind and meet fear, uncertainty and frailty with resolve.

'Devamitra has written a compelling book about his cancer journey that straddles a wide range of emotions: gruelling, funny, poignant and uplifting. You are drawn into his world as he undergoes particularly challenging treatment, whilst always maintaining a uniquely wry, even amused, perspective on life and death.' – Vidyamala Burch, co-founder of Breathworks, author of *Living Well with Pain and Illness* and *Mindfulness for Health*

'This is a remarkable book – honest, lucid, unflinching, funny and radical in its willingness to confront the facts of life and death. Devamitra tells the story of prostate cancer, and how his Buddhist practice met the challenges of diagnosis and treatment, even how cancer led to the deepening of his practice and his love of life.' – Maitreyabandhu, author of *Life with Full Attention* and *The Journey and the Guide*

'Quite often stories about cancer are framed in terms of a battle. This isn't always helpful, as it implies that disease progression means defeat or failure. Devamitra frames his account with interweaving themes of struggle, victory and setback, but also of calm and insight. We hear this story flavoured with his deep engagement with Buddhist teachings and practice, and his devotion to his teacher.' – William Stones, Professor of Obstetrics and Gynaecology and researcher in global health

'Who would have thought that having cancer could be so instructive, and at times so amusing? Devamitra writes of his experiences with a style unique to him: beautifully crafted, engaging, witty, poignant, reflective and always disarmingly honest. Devamitra faces his test as a Buddhist, but he wears his Buddhism lightly, even though it is Buddhism that guides him through it.' – Subhuti, author of *Mind in Harmony*

ISBN 978 1 911407 88 1
£12.99 / $18.95 / €14.95
224 pages

It's Not Out There
How to See Differently and Live an Extraordinary, Ordinary Life
Danapriya

Most of us constantly look outside ourselves for something: happiness, love, contentment. But this something is not out there. 'It' is within us. We are full of these qualities: happiness, love, contentment and more.

In *It's Not Out There*, Buddhist teacher and mentor, Danapriya, helps you to look inside yourself in such a way that life becomes more vivid, joyful and extraordinary.

If you want to suffer less and to live life more fully, this book is for you. It's about seeing the reality of the human predicament, and seeing through the illusions that create unnecessary pain for yourself and others. This book uncovers the fertile ground of your own potential, and enables you to live the life you are here for. Stop, look, listen and sense, you are worth it.

'Written in simple, down-to-earth language, It's Not Out There *is brimming with practical wisdom. Positive and encouraging, Danapriya shares ways to help anyone who wants to change their life and find greater happiness and fulfilment.'* – Dr Paramabandhu Groves, co-author of *Eight Step Recovery: Using the Buddha's Teachings to Overcome Addiction*

'Reading this book is like having a conversation with a wise friend – someone who doesn't just talk at you but who is interested in your thoughts and experience too. Buy one for everyone you know who is serious about life and how to live it well.' – Subhadramati**,** author of *Not About Being Good*

Born Ian Dixon in 1959, Danapriya ('one who loves giving') has been involved in personal growth and healing work for over three decades. Ordained into the Triratna Buddhist Order in 2001, he founded the Deal Buddhist Group in Kent, UK, in 2007. Based there, he continues to lead retreats and teach meditation, while also running the counselling business *Talking Listening Clarity*. www.danapriya.org

ISBN 978 1 911407 59 1
£9.99 / $13.95 / €11.95
160 pages

Uncontrived Mindfulness
Ending Suffering through Attention, Curiosity and Wisdom
Vajradevi

Uncontrived Mindfulness is a fresh and comprehensive guide
to awareness of how the mind shapes experience. The Buddha
emphasized that happiness is found through understanding the mind
rather than getting caught up in sense experience. This simple yet
radical shift is key to a relaxed and uncontrived way of practising.
Freedom comes from uniting right view and mindfulness.

A deep dive into the practice of exploring our experience as it
happens, Vajradevi's emphasis is on cultivating wisdom, using the
tools of attention, curiosity and discernment to recognize and see
through the delusion that is causing our suffering.

Vajradevi is a warm and insightful guide to this exploration,
drawing on her intensive and wide-ranging-practice of satipaṭṭhāna
meditation. The clear explanations and instructions are amplified by
Vajradevi's personal accounts, charting her uncompromising voyage
into self-discovery. Guided meditations are included.

*'Vajradevi is a practitioner who shares her own experience of practising
mindfulness simply and clearly. She makes traditional concepts accessible
because she knows them from the inside, and this book is full of stories of how
Vajradevi has learned to be mindful of her own life.'* – Vishvapani Blomfield,
author of *Gautama Buddha: The Life and Teachings of the Awakened One*

*'A wonderful book, written with that independence of mind characteristic
of deep practitioners.'* – Kamalashila, meditation teacher and author of
Buddhist Meditation: Tranquillity, Imagination & Insight

*'Vajradevi gives relevant and real examples which show us that dedicating
ourselves to mindfulness does not mean being cut off from life. I loved
reading the stories she weaves in to explain her journey in mindfulness and
the thoughtful connections she makes with common doubts or questions
about the practice, the journey, and its effects.'* – Ma Thet, translator for
Sayadaw U Tejaniya

Vajradevi met the Dharma at the age of 23. She was ordained into
the Triratna Buddhist Order in 1995. She leads retreats in the UK and
Europe that teach mindfulness as a path to wisdom.

ISBN 978-1-911407-61-4
£14.99 / $19.95 / €16.95
248 pages

The Burning House
A Buddhist Response to the Climate and Ecological Emergency
Shantigarbha

We are living in an age of climate and ecological emergency. Buddhist teacher and Nonviolent Communication trainer Shantigarbha suggests practical ways to make a difference. With personal stories, examples and guided reflections you will learn to work with doubt, overwhelm, grief and anger; engage with the science of the climate debates; free yourself to align with life; and act with courage, humour and generosity.

'One thing is certain: no meaningful systemic change in response to the ecological and climate emergency faced by all planetary life will be possible without a shift in human consciousness. This beautifully crafted, accessible book skilfully weaves Buddhist teachings, the author's personal journey and a passionate political and ethical commitment to an empathic path of transformation.' – Anna Grear, founder of the Global Network for the Study of Human Rights and the Environment (GNHRE); Editor in Chief *Journal of Human Rights and the Environment*

'How can Buddhism help us understand and respond to the greatest challenge that humanity has ever faced? Shantigarbha provides a welcome and very accessible introduction to the relevant teachings and how to embody them in our practice and activism.' – David Loy, author of *Ecodharma: Buddhist Teachings for the Ecological Crisis*

'The ecological crisis is nothing if not a spiritual crisis, a crisis of meaning and direction for our civilisation. The Burning House *is approachably written, and abides by the precautionary principle: moving as we are in a fog, it behoves us to slow down. Take a pause, and read this book.'* – Professor Rupert Read, author of *This Civilisation Is Finished*, and former student of Thich That Hanh and Joanna Macy

'For so many years now, we have heard the alarm of the climate and ecological emergency sounding, telling us that the house is on fire. If, like so many of us, you are uncertain what a Buddhist response to the climate emergency would look like, you will find Shantigarbha's book very helpful indeed.' – Vajrashura, Dharma teacher in the Triratna Buddhist Community

ISBN 978 1 911407 75 1
£9.99 / $15.95 / €12.95
272 pages

Introducing Mindfulness
Buddhist Background and Practical Exercises
Bhikkhu Anālayo

Buddhist meditator and scholar Bhikkhu Anālayo introduces
the Buddhist background to mindfulness practice, from mindful
eating to its formal cultivation as *satipaṭṭhāna* (the foundations of
mindfulness). As well as providing an accessible guide, Anālayo
gives a succinct historical survey of the development of mindfulness
in Buddhism, and practical exercises on how to develop it.

*'A wise and helpful presentation of essential elements of the Buddha's
teaching . . . it will be of great value for those who wish to put these
teachings into practice. A wonderful Dharma gift.'* – Joseph Goldstein,
author of *Mindfulness: A Practical Guide to Awakening*

*'A gold mine for anyone who is working in the broad field of mindfulness-
based programs for addressing health and wellbeing in the face of suffering
– in any or all of its guises.'* – Jon Kabat-Zinn, author of *Meditation Is
Not What You Think: Mindfulness and Why It Is So Important*

*'Bhikkhu Anālayo offers simple skilled mindfulness practices for each of the
dimensions of this book. Open-minded practices of embodied mindfulness
are described, beginning with eating and health, and continuing with
mindfulness examining mind and body, our relation to death, and the
nature of the mind itself. Significantly, by highlighting the earliest
teachings on internal and external mindfulness, Bhikkhu Anālayo shows
how, individually and collectively, we can use mindfulness to bring a
liberating understanding to ourselves and to the pressing problems of
our global, social, modern world. We need this more than ever.'* – Jack
Kornfield, from the Foreword

ISBN 978 1 911407 57 7
£13.99 / $18.95 / €16.95
176 pages